D0934189

ADOPTING OLDER CHILDREN

ADOPTING OLDER CHILDREN

ALFRED KADUSHIN

Columbia University Press

NEW YORK AND LONDON

*Alfred Kadushin is Professor of Social Work
at the University of Wisconsin.*

*To my Parents
Philip and Celia*

ISBN: 0-231-03322-2
Library of Congress Catalog Card Number: 71-125918
Printed in the United States of America

PREFACE

This book is a report of a courageous experiment conducted by a group of adoptive parents. These parents accepted a child for adoption when the child was five years of age or older. The book presents, primarily in the parents' own words, some of the joys and satisfactions, some of the sorrows and disappointments that resulted from welcoming the older child into the family. Happily the experience proved to be considerably more satisfying than disenchanting for the adoptive parents.

But while the people whose interviews are recorded here were adoptive parents, their experience speaks to that of all parents. A child is a child, biological or adopted; a parent is a parent, biological or adoptive. The living experience of parents caring for, protecting, loving, educating, and worrying over their children is fundamentally similar whatever the differences regarding the genesis of the parent-child relationship.

The fact of adoption may place the parent in a position which makes him somewhat more articulate about the experience of parenthood. A perceptive adoptive parent interviewed for the study noted that one of the differences between an adoptive parent and a biological parent was similar to that between a native-born and a naturalized citizen. The biological parent takes his parenthood for granted, as does the native his right to citizenship. Consequently, he may not give parenthood much thought. But since the adoptive parent has earned parenthood as a result of a social, legal procedure, rather than having it conferred automatically, he is required to be more self-conscious of his parenthood. This may make him more explicitly aware of what parenthood means to him, the gratification and fulfillment it offers, the disagreeable, regretful price it exacts. Being more self-conscious of parenthood, the adoptive parent can help all parents in clarifying the experience they share. Consequently, while having significance for adoptive parents in particular, the book has significance for parents in general.

The study reported here was conducted with support of a research grant from the Children's Bureau, U.S. Department of Health, Education, and Welfare. We should like very much to express our appreciation to the Children's Bureau for the support which made possible this study. We should like further to express our appreciation to The Division of Children and Youth, Wisconsin Department of Public Welfare and to its director, Frank Newgent, for permitting us to conduct the study in their agency, to Mary Code, research associate and fellow interviewer, to Katherine Ostrander and Lucille Rowley, typescript readers, and to Martha Fager, record reader. Without the courteous assistance and warm cooperation of these people the study could not have been undertaken or completed. But above all we thank the adoptive parents who welcomed us into their homes and shared some of the pleasures and pain of their adoptive experience with us.

ALFRED KADUSHIN

May 1970

CONTENTS

Chapter 1

ISSUES IN
ADOPTION OF
OLDER CHILDREN

Adoption involves becoming a parent through a legal social process rather than through a biological process. For the child, adoption involves a permanent change in family affiliation. Adoption provides permanent substitute care for the child when his own natural parents are unable, or unwilling, to care for him, and when these parents have been legally freed of any ties to the child. Adoption is the only procedure available which permits the child complete membership in a "substitute" family unit. As a result of the adoption, parents and children assume the same rights and obligations toward each other that exist between the nonadoptive parent and child. The effect of adoption is to create a new parent-child unit.

In different times, in different places, adoption has served different purposes. For the ancient Greeks and Romans adoptions were arranged to acquire an heir, to perpetuate the family name, and to give continuity to a family line. In India, adoptions could provide a male child in order to meet the demands of religious ceremonials. The adopting father declares, "I accept Thee for the fulfillment of religion; I take Thee for the continuation of lineage." Similarly, another ancient text notes that adoptions met the need for a male child since "Heaven awaits not one who has no male issue" (31, p. 110).

Adoption among primitive groups was often for the purpose of making a captive, or a member of an "out-group," a member of the "in-group" of the tribe, thus enhancing the economic and military power of the captors. Perpetuation of the family name and continuity of the family line were also motives for adoption among primitive groups. Among South African tribes it is said that when "The head of a krall passes away without leaving a son—his village has departed, his name is broken" (31, p. 106).

In the early history of adoptions the emphasis in the codes and legal arrangements indicated a primary concern with parents' rights and interests. More recent adoption legislation centers on the protection of the child as the paramount concern. What characterized adoptions in earlier periods of our history and distinguishes such adoptions from the current point of view, is that earlier the institution existed primarily to meet the needs of adults. The institution is supported today primarily because it meets the needs of children. We have moved from an orientation centered on providing children for childless parents to that more concerned with providing parents for parentless children.

However, the adoption must serve a significant purpose for the prospective adoptive parents; it must, in anticipation, fulfill a significant need, otherwise they would not voluntarily involve themselves in the process. For most prospective adoptive parents who, for one reason or another, cannot have children biologically, it is the preferred way of completing the family. The predisposition is, however, to imitate nature; to simulate the usual family situation. Since the biologically capable parents "acquires" the child at infancy the prospective adoptive parent, for these and other reasons, would like to acquire the adoptive child in early infancy. This brings us to the problem which is the central concern of this book.

The number of completed nonrelated adoptions has been increasing steadily.* In 1945 there were 28,000 such adoptions; in 1967, 83,700.

A nationwide summary of statistics from states reporting such information indicated that, in 1967, the median age of children at time of adoptive placement was 2.1 months; 85 per cent of all children adopted by nonrelatives are placed for adoption at less than 1 year of age (84, p. 9).†

For adoptive purposes the child who has reached the age of 5 is "overage." Few adoptive applicants come to the agency with an initial preference for accepting the "adoptable" child over 5 years of age. The older child is repeatedly identified in the adoption literature as "hard-to-place,"—or, euphemistically, "a child with special needs" (6, 9, 12, 18, pp. 24–27, 37, pp. 19–25, 60, 75, 77).

Adoptive parents seek to simulate the experiences of biological parents as closely as possible. Consequently, they want to adopt a child as young as possible. The older child comes to the adoptive home with some established patterns of dealing with the routines of daily life and with some emotional ties to previous parent figures. The adoptive parents must, in some measure, accept the child as he is in his differences from their own patterns. They must compete with memories of earlier affectional attachments. The older child is, supposedly, a damaged child. He is different from the infant available for adoption in that he is more likely to have experienced deprivation

---

* About half of all the adoptions which take place are relative adoptions, i.e., the children of a divorced woman are adopted by her second husband, an aunt and uncle adopt an orphaned nephew, etc. Our concern is with nonrelative adoption—children who are adopted by parents unrelated to them in any way.

† References are at the end of the book.

and discontinuity of mothering, the trauma of separation, and a sense of rejection and loss. The older the child, the older the emotional problems which result from such pathogenic experiences, and the more resistive such problems are to change. Such considerations make adoptive applicants hesitant to accept an older child.

During the 1940s and the 1950s there was a sizable number of prospective adoptive applicants for every white infant available. This ratio has been variously estimated from 4–5 to 8–10 applicants for one child. During this period an applicant anxious for a child and concerned about his acceptability to the agency, might have strategically moved to heighten his chances by suggesting to the agency that he was ready to consider adopting an older child (38).

More recently the supply and demand factors in the adoptive "market" have changed so that there is less need for an adoptive applicant to do this. While the number of adoptive applicants has been increasing, the supply of babies available for adoption has been increasing at a greater rate.

The ratio between the number of adoptive applicants and adoptive children in 1962 was 122 applicants for every 100 adoptive children (35, p. 739). While this includes children available at all ages it reflects the changing adoption situation in favor of the applicant. The result is likely to be a reduction in the number of applicants ready to take an older child for adoption and a consequent increase in the number of such children who are "adoptable" but "unplaceable."

The problem is likely to be compounded by the fact that there is an increasing tendency on the part of state legislatures to provide for termination of parental rights in the case of children in long-term foster care who have remained unvisited and ignored by their natural parents over a long period of time and where the likelihood of the child's return to his own home is minimal (65, pp. 11–15, 66, pp. 1–4).

A large proportion of children in foster care have been identified as having such a relationship with their natural parents. A nationwide study of children in foster care concluded that in "no more than 25% of the cases in most of the nine communities studied was it probable that the child would return to his own home. These children are 'orphans of the living' " (52, pp. 379–80).

Neglected children whose "own" parents' parental rights have been terminated form the largest group of older children needing adoption. The legislation noted above is likely to increase the number of such children. All of this suggests an intensification of a situation which is tragic for the child, expensive for the community, and impoverishing for some potential prospective parents. The child is denied full membership in a family group, with all this implies for happy, healthy, normal development. The community is faced with the responsibility of supporting the child until he achieves independence. The prospective adoptive parent might be denied some of the special satisfactions which come from adoption of an older child—if such special satisfactions do indeed exist—or he may be denying himself the opportunity for adoption because he hesitates to accept the older child.

The profession of social work has been given the particular responsibility, by society, for concern with the problems of parentless children and childless parents. The profession, therefore, has concern with the older child who needs a home and family. It has the responsibility for finding such homes and for selecting a particular home for a particular child. But the process begins with recruitment of a sufficiently large pool of adoptive parents interested in the older adoptable child.

In summarizing the experience of an agency which has developed a special adoptive program for the older child Brown notes that "certain factors stand out as 'musts'—foremost is the need for deep conviction by staff and board that these children can be placed—conviction is, therefore, our keynote" (9, p. 25). It was felt that if, as a result of the proposed research, it could be demonstrated that adoption of the older child is, for many, a successful adventure, this might help provide a broader empirical base than was previously available for developing conviction in such adoptive placements on the part of social workers. Such information might enable the worker to encourage the prospective adoptive parent who was interested in, but doubtful about, adopting an older child. It might also increase the number of people interested in such adoptions.

Having recruited adoptive parents for such children the social worker faces additional responsibilities. One lies in the area of anticipatory socialization to the role of parent. The worker helps the prospective adopter to increased understanding about the changes involved in the assumption of the role of parent, to accept the social and emotional consequences of such changes, to consider optimum adaptations to such changes, and to revise expectations of satisfactions so that they are realistic. The social worker is, however, handicapped in discharging this responsibility because of a lack of knowledge of problems and satisfactions in the adoption of older children.

If the social worker is to carry out effectively the responsibility of "educating" the client to the role of adoptive parent of the older child, she needs to be knowledgeable about the stress this role imposes, the nature of the possible desirable adaptations, and the satisfactions which might realistically be anticipated. She has to be more "expert" than the adoptive parent in her understanding of the situation, and the profession must provide the worker with such knowledge. It was hoped that a study of the experiences of adoptive parents who had accepted older children would yield more detailed information about such adoptions than is currently available.

The problem has some potential theoretical significance as well as significance for social work practice. Children who become available for adoption when older generally have been seriously deprived emotionally as well as physically during their infancy and early childhood—the most crucial developmental years. Adoptive homes, selected by the agency after considerable study, generally offer the child a reasonably healthy environment for growth and development. A study of the outcome of such adoptions would help to determine the reversibility of the effects of prolonged deprivation in early life.

Chapter 2

————◄◆►————

WHAT WE STUDIED

AND WHY

We selected for our study children who were white, mentally and physically normal, and who, at the time they were placed in the home of adoptive parents, were at least 5, but less than 12 years old. Children who met all of these requirements but who had been in the home on a foster care basis prior to adoption were not included in the study. For the sake of uniformity all children selected had been placed by the same state agency during the 10-year period 1952–1962. A review of the agency files indicated that there were a total of 112 families who, over the 10-year period, had completed the legal adoption of such a child.

We could not reach 17 of the families for various reasons. Permission to review the records and contact the families was requested of the local county judges; in only one case were we refused such permission. We were unable to locate 12 of the families who had adopted children some 6–10 years prior to the initiation of the study. Four families had moved and were not available for interviews.

Of the 95 families we reached, only 4 refused our request to visit and talk with them about their experience—a refusal rate of 4.2 per cent, which is comparatively low for adoption follow-up research. A high percentage (77 per cent) of the families we contacted by both phone and letter were unhesitatingly willing to see us—many going to great efforts so that both the adoptive father and mother would be home when we were to come. One father rescheduled a business trip, others arranged to take off from work early. In two instances we interviewed the father at his place of business and the mother joined us there. Typical responses to our request over the phone were, "Sure," "O.K.," "We'll be glad to see you," "We will be happy to talk to you."

Several parents mentioned that they were a little chagrined that the agency had not followed up from time to time to see how the adoption was working out. They were anxious to share their experience, but had little formal opportunity. The interviews presented a unique opportunity to talk to a knowledgeable, interested stranger about a subject of great meaning and emotional significance to the parents. Assurance of confidentiality permitted the parents to talk about their relationship with their children in an uninhibited fashion and at great length.

The families who had experienced less satisfaction in the adoptive experience (as determined by an analysis of the follow-up interview) were, with a few exceptions, just as eager to talk to us as were those who had a more successful experience. They seemed ready to share their story with the agency through the researchers. This was, possibly, a cathartic opportunity for them. It was also a chance to obtain absolution and reassurance about their possible contribution to the adoptive difficulties from an official source. It might have been seen as a possible entrée to help. One might even speculate about the opportunity it presented to express hostility toward the agency which was, in part, responsible for the adoption.

The adoptive parents' reaction on the telephone to requests for an interview was recorded verbatim. This material was then categorized in terms of levels of readiness to participate in the project. The distribution of responses is presented in Table I.

Table I   Response to Request for Interviews

Response	Number
Positive (unhesitatingly willing, no questions other than procedural, made effort to accommodate their schedule to that of interviewer, expressed eagerness) (Based on phone interview)	73
Positive Ambivalent (willing for the most part but some substantive questions raised about the research, initial response somewhat hesitant, guarded, little or no effort to accommodate their schedules but presented no difficulties) (Based on phone interview)	10
Negative Ambivalent (hesitant, doubtful, guarded, resistant, many substantive questions raised, consent with reluctance, need much reassurance, raise difficulties about appointment time) (Based on phone interview)	3
Negative (refused consent) (Based on phone interview)	4
Granted interview (letter contact only)	5
Total	95

An effort was made to determine if the small group of four families who refused was distinguishable in any way from the larger group who had been willing to grant the interview. Nothing in the background material of the children or in the original adoption studies suggested reasons for refusal. However, in two of the four refusals the parents hinted, in their telephone conversation with us, that the adoption had been unsuccessful.

In recapitulation, then, we started with 112 families who met all of the conditions for inclusion in the study group: 12 could not be located, 4 had moved from the state, permission to interview was refused by the county judge in 1 case, and 4 families refused to permit an interview. Of the original group of 112 families, interviews were ultimately held with 91 families who were eligible, located, available, and willing.

Sources of Data

The principal sources of data were the agency record material and the follow-up interviews with the adoptive parents. A less significant source of data were the parents' response forms completed after the formal interview.

RECORD MATERIAL

The first step in data collection was to summarize the significant background material. Four sets of records were reviewed. Generally separate records on the child's natural parents, on the child placed for adoption, and on the adoptive parents were available. In the case of the many children who came from families in contact with local welfare agencies prior to the state's assuming custody for the child we reviewed that agency's record of the family. Data were systematically collected through use of forms compiled on the basis of a preliminary review of a sample of the records.

The records were reviewed and the forms completed by two social workers with considerable agency experience, one of whom is a graduate of a school of social work. The project director, a graduate social worker, reread a 10 per cent sample of all of the records and independently completed a second set of forms to check the reliability of the information collected by the two record readers.

From the hundreds of pages of record material on each case we xeroxed pertinent statements and inserted them at appropriate points on the form. For instance, the following recording by the worker of the clients' reaction to the idea of adopting older children was xeroxed.

He and his wife have approached the idea of adoption very thoughtfully and are prepared to take one or two older children. They both realize that because of the wife's age they will not be able to have an infant placed with them. Mrs. B. talked about the age of children she would feel most comfortable with. She said that while she liked infants, she was sure that it would be a mistake for her to take a small child because of the age she would be when the child was an adolescent. Mrs. B. raised questions about the actual court procedures after I had made some interpretation as to the need to keep confidential the identity of natural parents and the location of the child from the natural parents. This they recognized would be harder if a child were older, and she seemed relieved to know that all of the dealings around adoptions would be with the agency and not with the family.

Such data reveal some of the qualitatively important individual situations that underlie regularities revealed by statistical material. It further permits checks on the reliability of researchers' categorizations without the need for full record review.

FOLLOW-UP INTERVIEW

The principal source of follow-up data was the semistructured interview with the adoptive mother and father following an interview guide. A preliminary interview guide was revised after interviews with 3 adoptive couples. In preparation, the interviewers role-played interviews with each other to gain familiarity with the guide. All of the interviewing was done by the author and one other interviewer. Both are graduates of a school of social work and have at least 15 years professional experience. The work was divided geographically.

In 77 cases (85 per cent) we interviewed father and mother together. In 12 instances (13 per cent) only the mother was available, and in 2 instances only the father. The child was out of the home during 66 (73 per cent) of the interviews; in 6 (7 per cent) instances the child was at home but out of sight and hearing. In 7 (8 per cent) instances the child was at home within hearing range and in 11 (12 per cent) additional cases was in and out of the room intermittently.

We attempted to tape record all the interviews. Only 4 couples refused. Our experience supports the general conclusion of other studies that interviewees are not reluctant to accede to taping, and that its effects on the interview are transient and not particularly significant.*

PARENT RESPONSE FORMS

In an effort to get at kinds of responses perhaps not freely offered in the interview, each parent was asked to complete a form at the end of the interview, before the interviewer left. In the few cases where this was inconvenient for the parents we requested that the forms be mailed to us. The principal unit on this form presented the parent with a series of incomplete sentences to which the parent was free to respond in any way, for example, "An adoptive family is _____."

"As an adoptive parent, I wish I had _____";

"When you adopt an older child _____."†

Parents were, on the whole, conscientious about completing the form. For many it was a task. The form was filled out completely or with few omissions by 122 parents (67 per cent).

The average interview ran between 2 and 2½ hours. Given the usual preliminaries, time for setting up the tape recording, time spent in waiting for completion of reaction forms, the usual total length of time spent in the home was 3 to 3½ hours.

* See "Tape Recording of Interviews in Adoption Research," A. Kadushin, *Journal of Jewish Communal Services*, Vol. 43, Summer 1967, pp. 327–34, for details regarding tape recording of these research interviews.

† This form was an adaption of one used in follow-up adoption research, by Professor David Fanshel, whom we thank for permission to use and adapt it.

The tapes of the interview were transcribed; they averaged 50 pages of double-spaced, typed material. Transcription of the more than 4,300 pages was in accordance with uniform instructions which required that the typist follow everything on the tape as faithfully as possible. Tapes were de-identified in transcription.

Rationale for Nature of Follow-up Data Collected

The principal focus of the interview and the response forms was the satisfactions and dissatisfactions, from the parents' point of view, in their relationship with the child. The child was not interviewed or studied except as he was reflected in what the parents offered. The rationale for such an approach needs, perhaps, to be spelled out.

Since many of the children in the study group were still quite young, it might be supposed that many were still resolving questions which concerned them regarding the adoption experience. It was felt that it might be an intrusion to enter their lives at this time of transition with a single interview covering questions of a highly sensitive nature.

The principal reason for interviewing parents only, however, lay in the rationale which was central to our approach. Studies of outcome in the social sciences have, most frequently, used as the criteria for determining levels of success some assessment of personality functioning. The subject lives through some experience—a series of interviews with a therapist, a period of hospitalization, a move to new housing, and so forth. He is then asked to complete some standardized inventory—the Minnesota Multiphasic Inventory (M.M.P.I.), the 16 Personality Factor Test, California Test of Personality, etc.—or some other procedures such as The Self Concept Q Sort is employed. The results of such "tests" are compared with the scores made by a control group—not subjected to the experience being studied—or are compared with the subject's own scores prior to engaging in the experience. The focus is most frequently on adjustment, intrapsychic functioning, or levels of psychological health.

An approach based on other criteria may be employed. The focus might be on social functioning and social role performance. The question of the subject's "adjustment" is here secondary to the satisfaction with which he performs his role according to the person who is his role reciprocal. "Objectively," in terms of some commonly accepted levels of interpersonal and intrapersonal performance, he may be judged to be doing poorly. However, in his own disorganized way he fits the needs and complements the requirements of his role reciprocal—the wife to the husband, the parent to the child, the employee to the employer.

Fanshel, in discussing the problem of measurement of outcome in adoptions research, makes a somewhat similar point. He notes that it would be a mistake "to equate *stress* in living experience with the *worthwhileness* of the experience for those involved" (emphasis in original; 22, p. 28).

For adoptive placement to be successful—that is, provide satisfaction to all parties in the relationship—it is not necessary that the child be "well adjusted" or "psychologically healthy." The child may not compare favorably with "normal" peers. Yet, whatever the child is, if the parents perceive him as acceptable to them, as being a satisfaction to them, the relationship has many strengths and is likely to endure.

One of the earliest studies of adoption follow-up noted the possible disparity between some objective assessment of the adequacy of "adjustment" according to community standards and parental satisfaction. Adoptive children in this study were evaluated as "capable" or "incapable"—"capable" children being those who were "law abiding, who manage their affairs with good sense and are living in accordance with good moral standards of their community." Some 28 (11.9 per cent) of the 235 children studied who were evaluated as "incapable" were "fairly well adjusted and suited to their rather unexacting environment." The author notes that "they may lack independence, resourcefulness and the ability to plan for themselves but they are not at odds with society. In general they are not disappointing to their adoptive parents; indeed some adoptive parents prefer the docile, quiet, unenterprising type of boy or girl to the more independent and self-reliant type. Some of them professed themselves quite satisfied with the way children, counted incapable, have developed" (80, p. 123).

The concept of complementarity, "A's behavior in acting out A's need X is gratifying to B's need Y, and B's behavior in acting out B's need Y is gratifying to A's need X" (89, p. 93), formulated in studies of marital interaction, is applicable to the relationship of adoptive parents to children.

Colvin has reported on studies which demonstrated that the best foster child-parent relationships were not necessarily those in which the parents formed the ideal picture of the good parent. "Instead it was strikingly evident that successful placements do occur with the correct matching of specific assets and defects on the part of both parents and children" (14, p. 46).

In examining the adoptive situation in the light of the social role relationships it is presumed that while it is possible for one party in the social role network to be satisfied and the reciprocal to be dissatisfied, this is unlikely. We are presuming that, if the child performs his role functions vis-à-vis the parent to the satisfaction of the parent, that this not only suggests reasonably decent adjustment on the part of the child but also that the child is satisfied in the relationship.

In any role network relationship one party may, of course, derive greater satisfaction; one party may exploit the other. But if the imbalance in satisfactions is persistent and pervasive the second party usually will make trouble. The unhappy child, denied essential gratification, in turn makes the parent unhappy by disobedience, destructive behavior, tantrums, school failure, withholding affectionate responses, enuresis, psychosomatic illness, food fads, compulsive rituals, and so forth. The child has a considerable armamentarium of responses at his command with which to defend his rights in the relationship. Parental satisfaction is likely, then, to be a sensitive, however oblique, indicator of the child's satisfaction in the relationship.

The correspondence between parental satisfaction and adoption outcome in studies which used measures more directly assessing the child's adjustment tends to support this contention. Thus Witmer says, "Parent satisfaction is one of the major criteria of adoption outcome." Lower ratings of satisfaction were associated with significantly lower ratings in terms of outcome (91, p. 393).

Another recent follow-up study of 200 agency adoptions further confirms the relationship. On the basis of intensive interviews with members of the adoptive family researchers made a global rating of family functioning. This was the principal criterion used in the study as a measure of success of the adoption. The factor "adoptive parent satisfaction in the adopted role" was very highly correlated (.69) with this outcome measure (43, p. 130).

This supports the supposition that there is an overlap in the two different types of criteria so that establishing the level of functioning in accordance with the mental health–personality adjustment criteria inferentially establishes a level of performance in accordance with social role functioning criteria. This is because psychologically "healthy" people are apt to perform their roles adequately. But if this is the case one can start with measuring the social role performance criteria and, inferentially, presume levels of function in terms of mental health–personality adjustment criteria.

Another argument supports the decision to interview parents only. Ultimately the research is meant to help adoption agencies to do their job more effectively by recruiting good adoptive homes for the children needing them. Given the reduction in emphasis on the obligation to the community that the married couple have children, the erosion of the religious duty to bear children, the increased social sanction, and availability, of satisfying alternative roles other than motherhood for women, it seems necessary, in turn, to increase emphasis on the personal returns, the personal satisfaction, the need fulfilling and self-actualizing aspects of parenthood. If adoptive parenthood proves to be a highly satisfying personal experience this fact can be reported to those who have never considered taking the step.

The child's adjustment, as a measure of adoption success, is a less appropriate criterion when limited adoption demand is a matter of concern. Agencies could previously center attention on the needs of the child and judge adoption in terms of whether or not it was adequately fulfilling those needs. The current balance between the supply of adoptive children and demands of adoptive parents requires more study of whether adoption is meeting the needs of the parents. The agency must be interested in adoptive child adjustment which presumes parental satisfaction; the prospective parent is interested in parent satisfaction which presumes child adjustment. The interests of all are largely congruent. The adoptive parents' needs and satisfactions are emphasized here to counterbalance the tendency of agencies to focus primarily and exclusively on the needs of the child. Adoption workers need to recognize the mutuality of needs and obligations among all family members.

The focus on parental reaction to the adoptive situation is consistent with the practice responsibilities of the adoption agencies. Prospective adoptive applicants have to be recruited for, and helped assume, the role of parents for the adoptable older children available. Such people would need to know about the experiences of other parents who adopted such children; they want to know, and need to be told, what difficulties they may encounter, what adaptations they might need to make, what satisfactions they are likely to derive. They would need help in viewing the experience not only from the points of view of the child and the social worker but first and primarily from the point of view of the parent group to whose ranks they are being recruited, and whose joys and disappointments they are being asked to share.

Chapter 3

———————◄◆►———————

THE

NATURAL

PARENTS

The child placed for adoption in infancy is, typically, an illegitimate child surrendered by his unwed mother shortly after birth. Thus 87 per cent of all nonrelative adoption (adoption by other than blood relatives) involves the illegitimate child (84). The child placed for adoption when he is 5 or older has a very different background. Typically this child is available for adoption as a result of court action instituted against the parents terminating their parental rights for neglect or inability to care for the child. This difference suggests that such children generally come from disorganized, multiproblem families and have suffered developmental and social deprivation over a number of years.

Socioeconomic Background of
Natural Parents

The background data from agency records on the family situation in which these children lived during infancy and early childhood substantiate these general contentions.

In 1960 about 43 per cent of all white adults had completed high school (85, Table 153, p. 120). However only 9 per cent of the natural parents had completed this much education (2 per cent of the fathers). Limited education is reflected in the occupational level of the natural parents. The greatest number, by far, are clustered in the unskilled and semiskilled categories: 82 per cent of the fathers for whom such information is available and 85 per cent of the mothers having worked in such jobs. From the limited educational attainments and associated low occupational skills of these parents it was to be expected that many of the families were living in, or on the edge of, poverty.

Social and Personal Difficulties

The problems of limited education, poor job skills, and consequent inadequate, precarious income were compounded for the many atypically large families in the group. Fifty-two (57 per cent) of the families from which these adopted children came had 5 or more children. The fact that less than 10.5 per cent of all American families in 1962 (85, Table 40, p. 242) had so many children as this suggests the burden of care and responsibility imposed on these parents. Some 15 per cent of the families were living in substandard, crowded housing.

These parents manifested considerable personal pathology which, in some measure, was the cause of the social problems the families faced but was also a result of the problems the families faced. Personal pathology included such conditions as mental deficiency, mental illness, emotional instability, alcoholism, promiscuity, and erratic work history. Thus some 31 per cent of the mothers and 21 per cent of the fathers were noted as emotionally unstable; 20 per cent of the mothers and 47 per cent of the fathers were regarded as alcoholic. We counted only those conditions for which there was clear and convincing substantiation in the record. A worker's overall evaluation, for instance, that the mother was unstable was not counted unless there was specific evidence for the assertion. The following is a report of a mother we counted as emotionally unstable.

Mother is "uniformly described as inadequate personality who lacks judgment, acts impulsively and is incapable of realistic planning or ability to profit from past experience. This is manifested by a record of 2 marriages, several pregnancies (different men), 5 arrests and conviction for prostitution, shoplifting, check forgery, obtaining money by false pretenses, fighting, suspicion of narcotics."

A recapitulation of the social and personal difficulties with which these families were struggling indicates that there was an average of 5.7 different, identifiable problems per family.

Many of these natural parents had experienced personal deprivation in their own childhood, 28 per cent of the group having such background histories. The record details some of this deprivation.

The mother has never known life in a secure and comfortable home. She herself was born out of wedlock. Her attachment to her own mother has never been strong and she had a stepfather at the age of about 2. She never felt wanted at home and left to go to work when she was 13. Married at 20, she bore 11 children in 16 years on the marginal, unstable income provided by an irresponsible husband who drank to excess.

A high percentage of these parents consequently had developmental experiences which impaired their capacity for parenthood.

Marital Situation

If one of the prerequisites for being a happy parent is having a happy marriage, few of these parents were so qualified. Of the families into which these children were born, the marriages of 41 per cent were initiated by premarital pregnancies—not the best start for a marriage. In the entire sample only 4 per cent of the marriages could be included in the category "parents living together harmoniously" during the major portion of the time the child was in the home before his first permanent placement; 69 per cent were checked: ". . . parents living together with considerable discord, arguing, fighting constantly. Marriage characterized by instability—pattern of brief separations, and/ or desertions—extramarital affairs."

A smaller percentage of families were broken during the major proportion of the time the child was in the home prior to first placement because one of the parents was hospitalized, imprisoned, had deserted, because the parents were divorced, or because the child was illegitimate and a family had never been established in the first place.

Descriptions of marital interaction in the records is almost uniformly negative.

They were always fighting. She said he drank to excess and was abusive. He said she was promiscuous.

He is cruel to his wife, he seems to needle her to get her upset and agitate her and belittle her. The quarreling and abusive language is upsetting and frightening to the children. He has given very little attention to his children. Mrs. F. feels more relaxed and at ease when Mr. F. is away. However, she misses her husband and doesn't know how she really stands with him. In spite of his cruelty and shortcomings she gets morose and tearful when he goes away and she thinks he might not come back to the family.

Parent-child Relationship

The records made clear the inadequate marital role performance of these parents. We assume that children are likely to be affected by an unhappy or conflict-ridden marriage.

The impact of the parents' relationship with the child is, of course, more direct and immediate. How adequately did these parents perform as parents?

Few of the natural parents were physically abusive or emotionally punitive toward the children. However, a large number of the mothers (70 per cent) were physically neglectful and/or emotionally neglectful (40 per cent): "Physically neglectful— child inadequately fed, clothed, health needs unmet, living conditions hazardous"; "Emotionally neglectful—parent indifferent, shows no affection, recognition, encouragement, approval of the child." In only 30% of the cases were the mothers regarded as normally warm and accepting ("concern for child expressed, parent shows affection, approval encouragement, acceptance, recognition"). After placement of these children in foster homes few parents visited regularly (12 per cent), wrote letters, and/or sent gifts regularly, and few planned regularly and realistically for the child's return home.

All of this indicates that the majority of these children were deprived of the kind of parental relationship generally regarded as essential for healthy emotional development, and that they experienced this inadequate parenting in the context of an unhappy marital situation.

Excerpts from the record material give a more graphic picture of the condition faced by these children in their childhood home. The records present a depressing, monotonously repetitive litany of inadequate care.

The child did not receive any regular medical care after his birth and the mother, who had 11 children in 15 years, paid little attention to him. He had the appearance of a tiny, wizened old man but he was strong and walked shortly after his first birthday. When removed from his own home his fingers, toes and genitals were frozen. Apparently the child received very little care. It was observed that pre-school siblings carried him around and he had to grab for his own food. No one particularly fed him. The mother had an IQ of 71 and had come to the attention of the Welfare Department some years earlier when she attempted to drown 5 of her children. Both the father and the mother were, at one time or another, institutionalized in a mental hospital, the father for alcoholism, the mother for simple schizophrenia.

In the case of neglect in this family of 8 children it was noted that some of the children were covered with severe heat rash and the doctor found crusting of the scalp with nits. The mother is described as having lapse of memory at times and it was not known whether this is due to lack of mature ability or because she is so worn out with having had so many children so close together. There are times when she seems quite confused. The father's employment record is very erratic and he has a record of absenteeism, irresponsibility, and considerable drinking.

The mother is an unhappy person and on psychiatric evaluation was found to be incapable of caring for her family. She herself was a deprived child whose father had died in an automobile accident when she was 4 and whose mother had died when she was 15. Married at 19, she had 9 children in 12 years. With increasing family responsibility, the marriage went down hill and this resulted in greater neglect of the children. The mother attempted to care for the children and outwardly showed affection for them but she was too immature and too overwhelmed to maintain a stable home. The house was described as filthy and unheated, the children were poorly clothed, truanted frequently, and were the victims of long standing physical neglect. There is evidence of a good relationship manifested by affection and compatibility.

The Public Welfare Department received many complaints about the neglect of these 11 siblings from neighbors, the city nurse and from the school. There is good evidence that the father beat the children often and sometimes mercilessly, and that he had an uncontrollable temper. The family of 13 lived in a 3-room shack barely big enough for 2 or 3 people. The children apparently did just about as they pleased and one child brought up another. Medical care was unheard of, meals were irregular, and the children were unclean, poorly clothed and malnourished. Neighbors reported that they felt sorry for the children who were begging for food in the neighborhood and took food into the home which they later learned had been locked up in the cupboard or refrigerator to be used by the parents in entertaining some of their adult friends rather than given to the children for whom it was intended.

An explicit effort was made to determine if the child had experienced a good relationship with a substitute parental figure during this early period of his life in his own home. Less than half of the children appeared to have had such a relationship, and the meaning of the relationship for the child, in most instances, is obscured by the paucity of material in the record. Grandparents played such a role in 23 per cent of the cases and older siblings in another 11 per cent.

Termination of Parental Rights

For most of these families difficulties in providing adequate care of the children had been a problem of long standing. For many there had been a series of complaints on the part of the community and sporadic intervention by welfare agencies, school authorities, public health nurses, and police officials. Action for termination of parental rights was initiated by the parent, or more frequently by "others," meaning some community agency, when it seemed clear to all who knew the situation that there was very little probability that the natural parents could provide the child with a viable, adequately functioning family.

The precipitating situation which led to legal action for termination of parental rights, whether initiated by the community agencies or by the parents, included such incidents as break-up of the marriage through divorce or desertion, the hospitalization or death of one or both of the parents, or imprisonment of one of the parents followed by the clear inability of the remaining parent to care for the children alone.

The following summaries indicate some of the situations which precipitated substitute care for these children.

The family of 9 children lived in marginal circumstances but the children were well cared for and no family friction was noted in the history. The parents were attached to the children and concerned about their welfare. After the birth of the 9th child it was discovered that the mother had a terminal illness with a very poor prognosis. The father, an unskilled laborer, was unemployed and receiving unemployment compensation at the time of the mother's illness and death. Unable to make plans for the children which would insure their continuing adequate care he accepted placement for them. While in placement he deserted and when brought back and sentenced for nonsupport he accepted termination of parental rights.

Mother of 9 children requested placement. The parents had previously been convicted and placed on probation for child neglect. The father had at this time left the state to find work in a neighboring state and assistance was denied the mother unless she would swear out a warrant against the father for nonsupport. The family was about to be evicted for nonpayment of rent. The mother, in requesting placement, declared that if the children's worker did not find homes for her children she would abandon them in the house in care of the 13-year-old boy (which she had done once before—verified) or else give them away to people who wanted children—that she could no longer fight the circumstances the care of the children incurred and was leaving Sunday to join her husband in (the neighboring state).

The situation precipitating the commitment to us (County Department of Public Welfare) was that the parents came and left the 4 children with their paternal grandparents promising to return for them and pay for their maintenance during this interval. Months went by and they neither returned nor did they communicate with the grandparents in any way. Because of family difficulties in the grandmother's home, because of the age of the grandparents and their state of health they are no longer able to keep the children. Attempts to locate the parents through relatives and other agencies have been unsuccessful.

Table II presents the principal reasons for action terminating parental rights to the children in the study group.

Table II   Principal Reason for Action Terminating Parental Rights of Natural Parents

Principal Reason	Number
Mother died, father deserted or could not provide care	12
Father died, mother deserted or could not provide care	4
Both parents died, institutionalized, or deserted	10
Mother hospitalized or imprisoned or deserted, father could not provide care or deserted	9
Father hospitalized or imprisoned, mother could not provide care or deserted	3
Father deserted, mother could not provide care	2
Marriage breaking up or broken, divorce contemplated or completed, neither parent wanted child	24
Gross neglect and/or abuse with one or both parents in the home	12
Mother unmarried and previous arrangement for care of child could not be continued	13
Other	2
Total	91

However the action for termination of parental rights was initiated, in only some 20 per cent of the cases were the parents actively opposed to the court action. In about 80 per cent of the cases parental rights were terminated with some measure of voluntary consent on the part of the parents.

It might be helpful to summarize the general impression derived from a study of the background material on these parents. They were, as a group, inadequately endowed and inadequately prepared for the heavy demands imposed upon them by life in a complex society. For some, limited intelligence potential was further depressed by a deprived and depriving environment in their own childhood. For others, whatever potentials they may have had were never actualized because of paucity of stimulation, inadequate resources, and truncated education. They therefore came to marriage and parenthood with limited capacity to earn a living, to support a family, and to deal competently with the interpersonal problem of marriage and parenthood. Nevertheless they seemed to have struggled and persevered against odds—odds which, for many of them became greater and greater, and more and more insurmountable, as child was added to child. Caught in a cycle, partly of their own making, partly made for them by circumstances which they were powerless to control, of increasing demands they were never capable of meeting, their frustration, resentment, unhappiness, and hostility kept mounting.

It would appear that they wanted to love their children, wanted to care for them. They had neither sufficient margins of physical and emotional strength and energy to be able to adequately care for their children. Their neglect was not willful, and it was probably with regret and some sorrow that they realized their failings as parents. There are few instances of deliberate physical abuse here; the sins visited by these parents on these children are, for the most part, sins of omission rather than sins of commission.

Many of them struggled with their failure as parents for a long time, and they were abetted by the reluctance on the part of the community to take action against parental rights except under the most clear-cut and egregious of circumstances. They tried to do the best they could—which wasn't very good— under conditions and pressures which would have guaranteed failure for many who, more fortunately situated, are contemptuously confident that they could have done better. They gave up their struggles, and gave up their children, with varying degrees of ambivalence, relief, guilt, and shame when some event made it manifestly impossible for them to continue—a mother died, a father was hospitalized, a parent deserted, the marriage broke up and both partners wanted a new start.

The picture presented by these families is substantially a replica of the configuration detailed by Young in her study of neglectful families (93). The assessment of blame and responsibility for what happened is a matter of secondary, or even tertiary, importance to the children; what does matter is that, for whatever reasons, the greatest percentage spent a considerable portion of their first years in a home characterized by marital discord and by physical and emotional deprivation, in contact with parents too busy, too inept, too unhappy, and too frustrated to give them the care they needed and to which they were entitled.

Chapter 4

THE

ADOPTED

CHILDREN

Identifying Data

In this chapter we shall attempt to present a general picture of the adoptive children included in this study. We have noted above that they were white, physically and mentally normal, and between 5 and 11 years of age at placement. In the final group, the total number of children with whose adopted families we conducted a follow-up interview was 91. Of these 49 (54 per cent) were boys; 42 (46 per cent) were girls. The mean age of the group at the time of adoptive placement was 7 years 2 months. The mean age at the time of the follow-up interview was 13 years 9 months.

We selected the limits of our age group to avoid children who had been placed at adolescence, because of the complexities which adolescent change might introduce into the study, but we were not able to avoid this problem. A considerable percentage of the children (58 per cent) were between 12 and 17 at the time of follow-up.

Children were selected for the study group only if they were of average or better intelligence; none achieved test scores of less than 80. Almost all (85 per cent) fell within the average (90 to 115) IQ range. One child was rated between 80 and 84, 3 between 84 and 89, and 5 above 115. The information is based on psychological test scores available in the child's record.

Placement History

Almost all of the children had some history in foster care between the time they were removed from their home and the time they were placed in an adoptive home. The age when the child first came into foster care is his earliest officially recorded experience with substitute care. This experience of separation from their own home took place at an average age of about 3½. They were placed for adoption at the average age of 7.2. The elapsed time between foster care and adoptive placement indicates that the child spent an average of about 3½ years in foster boarding home care.

During foster care the child was psychologically in limbo, belonging fully neither to his "own" family nor to the foster family, a period during which the child probably faced a problem of confused identification. Many were moved from one foster home to another for various reasons. While the mean number of placements for the group, *exclusive* of the adoptive placement, was 2.3, 31 children, 33 per cent of the group, experienced 3 or more foster home placements each. Table III summarizes the placement history of the children. The number of placements listed in the table includes the placement move to the adoptive home; stays of less than 2 weeks duration are not included.

Table III   Number of Placements Experienced by the Study Group Children

Total Number of Replacements	Number of Children
One	2
Two	30
Three	28
Four	16
Five	10
Six	1
Seven	2
Eight	0
Nine	2
Total	91

MULTIPLE PLACEMENTS

One clearly atypical aspect of the adoptive placement of the older child is that it is more apt to be a multiple placement. The older child, unlike the illegitimate infant, has generally come to the point of adoption as one of a number of siblings. For many of these children their siblings are important sources of emotional support. The agency needs to assess the advantages of adoption of the one older child against the disadvantages of divorcing the child from his siblings. Sibling deprivation has its consequences also. The agency tries, in the many cases where the sibling relationship has considerable meaning for the child, to solve the problem by making a multiple placement. Thus, in this study group of 91 cases, there is one instance of a placement of 5 children, one instance of a placement of 4 children, 3 instances in which 3 children were placed, and 34 instances where 2 children were placed for a total of 39 multiple placements—43 per cent of the total study group. In 26 of the 39 multiple placements more than one child was over 5 years of age. These 91 families accepted a total of 117 older children for adoptive placement.

Preparation for and Reaction
to Placement

The adoption literature suggests careful and gradual, which implies lengthy, preparation of the older child for adoption placement (4, pp. 327–34, 9, 13, pp. 10–16, 16, pp. 111–27, 27, 29, pp. 277–82, 41, 44, pp. 1–6, 49, pp. 3–8, 78). This is predicated on the need to resolve problems regarding the child's conception of his acceptability and to deal with already established affectional relationships.

Having experienced rejection at least once, and in many cases a number of times, the child is anxious about the possibility of experiencing rejection again. Hence, while he is anxious to move into adoptive care he is also fearful of the impending move. Having developed some ties to the last foster parents as well as to earlier parental figures he is concerned about the implications of disloyalty to them by making himself the child of new parents. All of this indicates the need for discussion between the worker and the child about adoption.

Such preparation is also predicated on the principle that the child should actively participate in the placement process. This is particularly true in adoptive placements of older children who have the capacity for such active participation. "Adoption is not something done *to* the older child but *with* the older child."

The literature also suggests, as part of such preparation, a gradual introduction of the child to the adoptive parents and the adoptive home (16).

In 90 per cent of the study group, records indicate that the agency carefully prepared the child for the move into the adoptive home. The records rarely provide the detail for an analysis of the process of preparation or its content. We have to be satisfied merely with the recognition that some kind of preparatory discussion took place between worker and child. This was also true of those worker-foster parent contacts devoted to helping the foster parents prepare for relinquishing the child. Summary recordings of such discussions allude to their concern with the meaning of adoption for the child, the meaning of change of name, discussion of the child's fears, and clarification of the future relationships between the child and the foster parent and the child and the worker.

Gradual introduction of the child into the home involved meeting with the adoptive parents out of the home—in the local park or restaurant—or a series of visits to the adoptive home culminating in the child's staying overnight, generally on a weekend. In some instances visits were few and brief, in other instances frequent and prolonged. The preparation process was often completed in a few days; once it took six weeks. The typical preparation program involved a series of two or three meetings between case worker and child regarding the impending move, one out-of-home visit, and one or two visits to the adoptive home before the move actually took place.

Readiness for adoptive placement on the part of the child is regarded as one of the crucial indices of probable placement success (44, pp. 1–6). The literature notes the following criteria as important in determining the readiness of an older child for placement.

1. Ability to adjust to loss of old parental ties and to accept new parental relationship. This implies some sense of trust in the adoptive parents' willingness to accept him (4, pp. 327–34, 44, pp. 1–6, 49, pp. 3–8, 78).

2. Emotional acceptance of the fact that he cannot return to his own parents and that this relationship cannot be revived (44, pp. 1–6).

3. Expression of explicit desire for adoption (41, 44, pp. 1–6).

4. Behavior which indicates motivation to adjust to the adoptive situation (44, pp. 1–6).

While the child may be ready, it is natural—as is true for people everywhere with regard to any significant situation—for some ambivalence to exist.

In 65 per cent of the cases the child was either positive or positive ambivalent in his response to the move. In only 18 per cent of the cases was he negative ambivalent, and in no case was he negative.

This, in retrospect, is to have been expected, since if the child had been strongly opposed to replacement, and had manifested considerable opposition, he would have been regarded as "unprepared" and the replacement either postponed or cancelled.

Since these children were old enough at the time of adoptive placement to be aware of what was happening, to participate in the process and to share verbally their feelings, reactions to the incident of placement were both verbal and behavioral. Most frequently it went smoothly—the children, as noted above, were anxious to go into permanent homes despite some ambivalence.

At one point, [child] mentioned that he wanted to come back to foster home at some future date but this was not replied to and passed over quickly with [child] seemingly forgetting the matter. The foster mother again reassured him that she wanted him to be happy and felt that he would be in his new home with his new father and mother and [child] seemed accepting of this. She gave him a big hug before he left and then he rather gaily skipped out of the house with no apparent fear or sadness showing. [Child] seemed eager to leave quickly and hopped into the car with hardly a good-bye.

He was very excited when we arrived and ran out of the car but first cautioned me to stay behind so he could enter the door alone. As he ran into the open door, he yelled, "I've come to stay." He immediately began showing his clothing articles to the adoptive mother and also some of the things which he had done at school. He seemed to be comfortable with her, though there was some over-activity as if he was under nervous tension and he had to keep well occupied.

[Child] seemed very accepting of the move and quite comfortable in the adoptive home. He showed enthusiasm over staying with them.

On occasion the ties to the foster home were sufficiently strong, and anxiety about what might be encountered in the new, strange home so great, that the move was made with more difficulty. The following reaction on the part of a seven-year-old boy is one of the responses categorized as negative ambivalent.

[Child] reacted quite negatively to the idea of placement and the move was made with considerable difficulty for him. The fact that [child] had a chance to visit and get acquainted with the adoptive parents did not seem to lessen his feeling of anger regarding removal from the foster home. Both on occasion of the visit and at the home at the time of placement [child] cried and was very angry and hostile toward the worker upon removal from the home, but following his temper outburst and tantrums over a five or ten minute period he then quieted and became more talkative and less angry and hostile.
However, once [child] was actually in his new adoptive home he was quite happy and satisfied and did not show anxiety or anger and it appears that he should adjust quite well in the new home.

We reviewed the records for material on strength and focus of the child's identification and of his emotional attachments by noting, throughout his placement history, factors which might relate to this. These were checked for any expression of desire to visit or write, to maintain communication with the natural parents, siblings in other homes, or previous foster families. We noted the extent to which he spoke or asked questions about such significant others in his life. In line with Weinstein's finding that "carryover of identification [with the natural parents] would seem to require periodic reinforcement through contact" (87, p. 52) we tried to tabulate data on frequency of contacts with natural parents and siblings. We looked for material related to the changes in the child's readiness to give up his own family name and to assume the family name of foster parents, and the readiness with which he transferred parental titles (mommy, daddy, momma, pappa, etc.) to his substitute parents. We attempted to record this information separately for each of the substitute homes in which the child had lived prior to adoptive placement.

The records suggest the beginning of a process essential to integration of the child into the adoptive family—the process of dissolution of the emotional ties to the child's "own" family. Most of these children began actively to forget their "own" parents during the foster care placement period.

The records indicate that by the time the children were placed in the adoptive home half of the group showed no overt signs of identification with their natural parents. There was evidence of more overt ties to siblings and to former foster parents.

Emotional Functioning

For each of the placements, we extracted information regarding the child's behavior in the home, the school, and the community. This suggests the child's personality strengths and weaknesses, problems and strengths in emotional and interpersonal functioning. This was done separately for each placement in an attempt to obtain some idea of changes in the child's functioning over a period of time.

Throughout the period in placement the children had each manifested an average of three specific, identifiable behavioral problems. In general the specific behavioral problems which the younger children displayed tended to diminish in severity as the child approached school age.

We included only behavioral manifestations which the record indicated were problematic. For instance, a psychological report on one child noted that "some slightly compulsive traits were observed in the need for accuracy, although this did not seem excessive for a boy in the early school age period." Compulsiveness, as a neurotic habit, was not, therefore, checked for this child.

Another criterion applied in tabulation was that of persistence with which the problem was manifested. If the child vomited once or twice in response to stressful situations we did not check this as a neurotic anxiety symptom. For instance one record read, "[Child] exhibited no real behavior problem during the 3 years in the foster home. There were occasional outbursts of negativism and mild temper tantrums but these seemed short-lived and rare."

Problems and improvements are illustratively noted in summary fashion in the following record excerpts.

Initial problems: first 6 to 8 months in home [child] *was enuretic and had poor eating habits. He was fearful of various animals in the dark, and was dependent upon his younger sister, placed with him in the foster home. As the placement progressed,* [child's] *enuresis ceased to be a problem* [6 to 8 months], *his eating habits improved* [1 year], *and he became less and less dependent on his sister. After about 1 year in placement* [4½ years old] *he became normally self-sufficient . . . in caring for himself, dressing, feeding, and was less fearful of the dark.*

[Child] *during early period of placement was described as fearful and insecure, also had enuretic problem. Was quite controlling of, and protective towards, younger sibling. His physical development was below average. As placement progressed he lost most of his fearfulness, showed gains in his feeling of security. For the most part enuresis stopped entirely except when undergoing emotional upset* [i.e., sibling visits]. *Domination of younger sibling less evident although it still continued to a degree. Continued to need considerable parental attention and affection.*

In Boehm's study of children in foster care one of the most significant findings was the increase in emotional problems with length in placement and the increased emotional impairment of children awaiting placement. In her group of 30 children awaiting adoption 72 behavior problems were manifested by 21 children at the time of study: an average of 3.5 problems per child (6, p. 11). The children in our study group manifested a total of 260 problems distributed among 91 children over the course of the total time in care (an average of 2.9 problems per child) but by the time of adoptive placement most of the symptoms had shown considerable improvement.

Behavioral symtomatology is one indication of the level of emotional functioning in the group of children with whom we are concerned. The ability to establish interpersonal relationships is another sensitive indicator of emotional functioning; it is also regarded as one of the principal criteria for the readiness for adoption (16, pp. 111–27, 45, pp. 107–12). We attempted a summarized categorization of the child's capacity to establish personal relationships with others. We were assisted in this by whatever psychological and/or psychiatric reports were included in the records and by the statements regarding the child's functioning prepared by the worker in writing the usual summarization for adoptive placement, a summarization which frequently included an evaluation of the child's capacity to establish a relationship with others. Table IV presents this information.

A large percentage of the children were perceived by the social workers who had contact with them as capable of establishing effective interpersonal relationship. This is congruent with the relative infrequency of emotional problems noted above. The favorable picture seems surprising for a group which had encountered what appears to be considerable situational and psychic stress. This unexpected finding is substantiated, however, by the data on referral for psychological and/or psychiatric examination. While 77 per cent of the children had been referred for such examination during their period in placement, only 4 per cent resulted from emotionally disturbed behavior. In most instances the referral was for a routine examination or specifically as an aid in placement planning.

Some part of the explanation for the level of the group's capacity to establish good interpersonal relations and the low incidence of emotional problems might lie with the requirements we applied in selecting our sample. We eliminated all

Table IV   Child's Overall Capacity to Establish Interpersonal Relationships

Level of Overall Capacity to Establish Relationships	Number
Good (good ego strength, ready to risk self in relationship with others, is warm, affectionate, emotionally responsive without significant transference elements)	21
Fair (shows ability to involve self with others but somewhat hesitant, diffident, needs some proof of his acceptance by others before ready to risk self, needs some encouragement but once is assured can move freely to involve himself, limited transference elements)	51
Doubtful (seems to have the capacity but it manifests itself infrequently and in highly favorable circumstances for self in a psychologically emotionally safe situation, needs considerable encouragement and prolonged proof of his acceptance by others before ready to risk himself. Given these conditions, however, he shows a capacity to relate to others; large component of transference)	17
Poor (cold, reserved, aloof, affectionateless, unable, or too threatened, to risk self, even under very favorable circumstances, in an emotionally safe climate)	2
Totals	91

older children free for adoption but regarded by the agency as poor risks because of the behavioral problems and emotional disabilities they presented. These children were never placed in adoptive homes and hence could not appear in our study group. We further required that legal adoption of the placed child should actually have been completed. This eliminated children whom the agency decided to place for adoption but who, for one reason or another, could not successfully achieve acceptance by the prospective adoptive parents during the trial year. Our study group might be regarded then as a rather select group, one criterion being, in fact, reasonably healthy emotional functioning.

How selective was this group of children?

A previous study (39, p. 101) on the hard-to-place child, conducted at the agency, would suggest that the children in this group were not highly selected. This earlier study consisted of all children for whom the agency had legal guardianship (which implied that they were available for adoption) for a period of 6 months or more on June 1, 1957, and who had not as yet been placed for adoption. The study covered an 8-year period and was designed to identify the factors delaying adoptive placement. While 102 of the 220 adoptable but unplaced children were between the ages of 5 and 10, in only 54 instances was age, per se, regarded as the primary deterrent to placement. The other older children presented additional factors—minority race membership, handicap, etc.—which reduced their placeability and delayed adoption to the point where they had "acquired" age as an extra handicap to placement. Thus, only 54 children might have been qualified for inclusion in the present study since they were white, physically and mentally normal, and over 5 years of age, but they failed to be included because they had not actually been placed for adoption.

The present study covers a 10-year period (1952–62); the earlier study covers an 8-year period (1949–57). In the 10-year period covered by the study the agency placed 150 white, normal children aged 5–11—the 91 children in the study group, 26 older siblings, 21 children in families who, for one reason or another, were not contacted, and 12 additional children who were placed but removed from the home before final adoption. In the 8 years of the earlier study, the agency failed to place 54 white, normal children between the ages of 5 and 10. While the 2 studies lack direct comparability, the available data tends to substantiate the contention that the group placed was not a highly selected minority of the total number of such children available for placement.

Chapter 5

THE

ADOPTIVE

PARENTS

Background Characteristics

One of the distinguishing characteristics of adoptive parents of older children is that, as a group, they are older than adoptive parents generally. The mean age of our adoptive mothers at the time of adoptive placement was 40 years; the mean age of the fathers was 41.5. Fifteen per cent of the mothers and 20 per cent of the fathers were 45 years or older at the time of adoptive placement. National figures do not include the age of adoptive parents at the time of placement. However, in a study of 9 American communities, Maas notes that typically the wife was about 34, the husband about 37 (52, p. 364).

The age of the adoptive parent is not considered as significant as the difference in age between the adoptive parents and the child. The agency would like, as much as possible, to simulate the natural situation. An effort is therefore made to achieve an age spread between adoptive parent and child which conforms to the age spread in the general population. They seek parents for children—not grandparents. To violate this increases the conspicuousness and visibility of adoption and may create problems. It also means that interests of parents and children are likely to be more divergent and that parents lack the sheer physical energy necessary to keep up with young children. Of greater importance is the fact that the agency would like to insure for the child the probability that the parent will live through his years of dependency. What is of significance, then, is not the age of the adoptive parent, per se, but the difference in age between adoptive parent and child.

The mean difference in age between the adoptive parent and child for this group at the time of adoptive placement was 32.5 for the mother and 34 for the father. If we can assume that most of the figures on age of adoptive parents available from other studies refer to parents who adopted infants of 1 year or younger we can see that, in terms of age difference, our group of adoptive parents is similar to adoptive parents of infants.

There is a clear difference between the socioeconomic level of the home from which these children came and the adoptive home in which they were placed. While only 1 per cent of the natural parents had any college education, 31 per cent of the adoptive mothers and 30 per cent of the adoptive fathers had some college education. While about 30 per cent of the natural fathers had failed to complete grade school, this was true of only 4 per cent of the adoptive fathers.

Using categories in the *Dictionary of Occupational Titles* (86), 62 per cent of the natural fathers worked at unskilled or semiskilled occupations; this was true for only 1 per cent of the adoptive fathers. Conversely, while none of the natural fathers were in a profession, this was the occupational grouping of 36 per cent of the adoptive fathers.

Since education and occupation are the two most sensitive

indicators of socioeconomic level, it can be seen that almost all the children were displaced upward when moved from their own homes to the adoptive homes.

Some 85 per cent of the adoptive parents are Protestants; so were the children's natural parents. The mean age of the marriage at the time of adoptive placement was 14 years.

Developmental History and Adult Functioning

We reviewed the record for any evidence of significant problems in the developmental history of the adoptive parents in order to obtain clues to problems in adoptive functioning. We looked for family breakdown during the formative years of either of the adoptive parents, a history of excessively strong attachment toward their own parents or, conversely, notable hostility toward parents, difficulty in heterosexual adjustment, or physical difficulties. We further attempted to explicate problematic areas in the life situation of the adoptive parents at the time of the adoptive study by checking occupational adjustment, finances, nonsexual reciprocal roles of husband and wife, difficulty with in-laws, health problems, relations with children already in the home, and so forth. The record noted few problems for these adoptive couples either in the material regarding developmental history or that regarding the situation at the time of the study. The picture is that of a stable group of people who apparently had no problems other than the usual vexations of everyday living.

There were some exceptions of course—15 per cent had come from a home broken by death, divorce, or some other contingency while they were children; 8 per cent had experienced difficulty in heterosexual adjustment; 4.5 per cent presented problems in the area of sibling or peer relationship; 4 per cent had experienced a divorce; 12 per cent had some problem either of overattachment or hostility in relation to their own parent. Several had had a mental breakdown, and one adoptive father had been rejected by the Army because of psychoneurotic anxiety.

This group represented the generation born during the Great Depression of the thirties, and in 14 instances (15 per cent) specific mention was made of economic deprivation as one of the difficulties they faced while growing up. As one father said, "We always had something to eat, but that's about all."

The general low percentage of pathology might have been anticipated. Applicants who presented considerable evidence of the difficulties for which we were looking would, in all likelihood, have been screened out by the agency. If they were accepted, and if the agency's presumption is correct (that such difficulties increase the possibility of adoptive placement failure) then, once again, they would not have shown up in our sample of families who had successfully hurdled the obstacles to legal adoption.

Motivation for Adoption

Most parents gave as reasons for having adopted a child that they enjoyed children, could not have any of their own, and had always wanted a family. This basic motivation received support from other, related, needs and desires—"to share our home and love with a child," "a wish to give to a child," "satisfaction in a dependent child now that our own were almost grown," "room in our hearts and home for a child," "fill some of the empty spaces in our lives," "enjoyment in watching a child grow and develop," "pleasure in drawing out what is inside a child and bringing out the stuff that was in them," "joy in seeing them make progress and grow into productive adulthood," "make our lives more meaningful," "more purposeful," "more enjoyable," "pleasure in knowing we are a part of a child's life," "that we belong to somebody."

Such "healthy" motives accounted for more than 90 per cent of the cases. In others the basic motivation of completing a family was associated with a desire to provide a sibling for their "own" child or a child previously adopted. These applicants still regarded their family as incomplete with only one child.

In 61 per cent of the cases the woman was either infertile or presented a history of repeated miscarriages and/or stillbirths at the time of adoptive application. In 10 per cent of the cases, the man was infertile. In a surprisingly large number of cases, 24 per cent, there was a failure to conceive but the cause of infertility was not clear. Here apparently the agency made a decision on pragmatic grounds. If a couple on the average of 40–41 years of age and married 10–15 years had not had a child it would seem that infertility was thus established.

Almost all of these couples had come to terms with their infertility—they had some feeling about it, but they had learned to live with it, it did not affect their behavior, and they could discuss it without undue hesitancy or defensiveness, resentment or bitterness. This, once again, might have been anticipated since very poor adjustment to infertility, with significant residuals affecting current behavior, might have dictated hesitancy in accepting the applicants as adoptive parents.

For most of these couples the knowledge of their infertility was nothing new. They had lived with the certainty of this, or a strong suspicion of this, for a long time. Habituation and time had dulled some of the pain.

Experience with Children

Almost all of the applicants claimed some experience as parental surrogates: 18 (20 per cent) had some professional experience in working with children as teachers, doctors, nurses, and so forth; 23 (25 per cent) had had volunteer experience with children as scout leaders, club group leaders, 4-H work, and church groups; 50 (55 per cent) claimed a special interest in neighborhood children, they took them on excursions or played with them in their back yards, or else they had cared for nieces and nephews for extended periods of time while the children's parents were on vacation or in the hospital; 12 (13 per cent) had experience as foster parents.

In 33 (37 per cent) of the cases, the applicants were already parents. These couples either had a child of their own or else had previously adopted a child: 18 couples had had children of their own; 15 had previously adopted a child.

Many in the group had, of course, more than one kind of experience with children. If the best preparation for adoptive parenthood is actual engagement in the substitute parental role, most of these couples had some such preparation—although there is of course a significant difference between being a full-time and part-time parent. Professional experience as teachers and volunteer experiences with scout groups, church groups, and 4-H groups was generally with the school age child, which made this particularly pertinent experience for the adoption of older children.

The large percentage of these parents coming to adoptive parenthood with experience indicates another atypical feature of older adoptions. The younger child adopted by younger parents is apt to be the first child adopted. The older child is adopted by older parents who frequently may have had a child earlier and subsequently become infertile, or who may have adopted a child previously. This is a significant complicating factor for the older child, since from the first he faces the problem not only of adjusting to a parent-child relationship but to a competitive sibling-sibling relationship as well.

Preparation for Placement

Just as the child requires preparation for the adoptive home the adoptive parent requires preparation to receive the child (18, 30, 45). The agency spends some time discussing with parents general problems they are likely to encounter and some of the specific problems in adopting an older child. The following specific topics came up for discussion between the adoptive parents and worker during the process of such preparation:

discipline—40 (44 per cent); attachment of child to previous family groups—52 (57 per cent); and reactions of "significant others" including "own" children—27 (30 per cent). Preparation also involves helping the parents accept the idea of adopting an older child.

Remarks about age preferences weave in and out of discussions of preferences regarding sex, ethnic background, disabilities in the child, and the child's family, etc. Further, it is hard to pin down because of changes in preference at different times during the adoptive study. We nevertheless attempted to categorize parents' attitude toward the idea of adopting the older child in records of later contacts in the adoption study.

Thirty-six per cent of the couples were categorized as having a "positive" attitude toward the idea of adopting an older child; they saw this "as a good thing; an older child being 'right' and 'natural' for them; they preferred an older child to an infant with little rationalization or defensiveness." Another 39 per cent were "positive ambivalent," that is "they were ready to accept an older child; they knew, in view of their age, that this is a good thing and that, in reality, they were not likely to be considered by the agency for a younger child; they accept the reality of the situation gracefully with little bitterness or resentment." This indicates that for the great majority of these parents the older adoptive child was an acceptable choice. This is the situation toward the end of the home study after, however, considerable "education" by the worker.

We can see this in parents' remarks during the follow-up interviews when recalling their thinking before the adoption. For many, the older child, while ultimately acceptable, was not their initial preference. This is congruent with what is generally noted in the literature about applicants' initial preferences as related to the older child.

Lyle, writing of a private agency which sought to place older children for adoption, points to the fact that few prospective adoptive parents came to the initial interview with a preference for an older child. This was true even of older applicants (49, p. 3). Hallinan seconds this when she states that "most adoptive couples, regardless of their own age, come to an agency with requests for infants" (29, p. 278) and this is noted by Fradkin as well (23, pp. 1–10).

Relatively few couples indicated in the follow-up interview that their initial preference had been for a child 5 or older. Some of these sought an older child, feeling it appropriate in terms of their own age.

FATHER: *Well, we really requested an older child . . . uh . . . we were older ourselves, that's mainly why . . . [laughs].*

FATHER: *We were more than ready to have a family and, realizing we had been married for a while, we were perfectly willing and ready to take older children. . . . So that's why we told the agency, naturally, that we would take from one to three, either sex, and any age. Up to . . . well, we had set an age limit of ten, hadn't we?*

MOTHER: *Yes.*

FATHER: *Up to ten. Yes, we felt we had some catching up to do as far as family was concerned.*

MOTHER: *It would have been possible, you see, we could have had a nine-year-old child. We had been married ten years.*

Some preferred an older child because of the age of a child already in the home and the desire for companionship for this child.

INTERVIEWER: *Well, uh, how did you happen to adopt a boy over five? What was the story on that?*

MOTHER: *We wanted one that age since our own child was, well, by the time . . . our own child was about eight. Or nine. So we asked for a child about six or seven.*

The realities of the adoptive applicant situation and the desire for a child dictated a shift in preference for some applicants.

A mother said, "I believe they told us that the waiting bit would be so much longer for a younger child, and if we'd prefer an older child the waiting bit wouldn't be too long."

MOTHER: *Well, uh* [laughs] *do you want to tell her or should I . . . . . yeah . . . we wanted children . . . we wanted to have children . . . actually older children seemed to be the only ones available for us . . . because we were older. . . . And in fact, to begin with, we hadn't thought about an older child. But as we got into it . . . we could see that they were the ones that were available and needed a home . . . and we had a home . . . so it just naturally. . . .*
FATHER: *And we couldn't see where it made any difference. . . .*

The process of change in preference was gradual.

FATHER: *Nope, we hadn't thought of it at first, what we first planned on was a preschool baby, was what we really wanted . . . but then after . . . we, ah, talked to this . . . Miss_____ wasn't it? She was out there for a long . . . for a good many, you know, quite a few times. . . . Well, it was the first time that we were in the office that they told us we were too old to . . . yeah, too old for a baby.*
MOTHER: *. . . . adopt a baby.*
INTERVIEWER: *I see.*
FATHER: *Then they started working on us for older children . . . and the more they talked, the more we thought about it . . . an'. . . . And it . . . I don't know what could a' worked out any better.*

And for some parents the full acceptance of the older child did not come until they were actually confronted with the living reality of a particular child that the agency was ready to offer them, and who appeared to be acceptable to them. Then age, per se, became a secondary consideration.

FATHER: *Well I tell ya . . . we still . . . we still had a mind that we would have liked someone younger. . . . However the possibility of our getting someone younger was growing less all the time . . . I mean, we were gettin' older and there was less possibility of our gettin' a younger child . . . so then we saw him and we. . . .*

MOTHER: *He was so cute. . . .*

FATHER: *Liked him as far as that goes . . . and we did feel that we didn't have too much chance of gettin' one much younger. . . . That's when we decided that probably we'd take him.*

INTERVIEWER: *Um huh. [Pause] When you saw him you reacted very positively to him.*

MOTHER: *Oh, goodness. . . .*

FATHER: *Oh, yeah, we liked him, very much. . . .*

While the older child was not initially preferred, the fact that preferences were flexible and subject to change supports Maas' finding that more applicants would accept older children than agencies recognize. Maas points to the fact that while 63 couples in his nationwide sample expressed willingness to accept a child of age 2 or older, only 33 such children were placed in adoption with these parents by the agencies, and the others received younger children (53, p. 20).

Evaluation of Applicants

In that the adoptive parent group presented little evidence of developmental pathology, was functioning with reasonable adequacy as adults, had an essentially healthy motivation for adoption, had in some measure resolved conflicts regarding infertility, and had developed some acceptance of the idea of adopting an older child suggests that these couples would be favorably evaluated by the agency.

Each of the adoptive records contains a summation of the impressions of the social worker who worked with the adoptive parents. Such statements were primarily favorable, as might be expected, since all the couples in the group had been accepted by the agency as adoptive parents. The composite portrait which follows might characterize about 90 per cent of these adoptive couples with reasonable accuracy. Each sentence is taken verbatim from workers' summary statements, and most appear repetitiously in one form or another in the records.

This couple seems to have sufficient ego strength to provide an environment which would offer a child the opportunity to develop socially and emotionally. While experiencing some problems in their own development the total picture, for both the adoptive mother and father, suggests that their own family experiences were essentially positive. They have achieved satisfaction in their marriage, although there are areas of disagreement. The marriage is a congenial relationship of both interests and responsibilities. Each of the partners is well identified with his own sexual role. The adoptive study suggests that they enjoy contact with children and reflects an understanding and acceptance of children. They are relaxed, flexible, and realistic in their expectations. They would tend to take into account a child's individuality in the demands they make of a child. While the adoptive parents could effectively handle any kind of behavior they could understand it is possible that behavior based on deep-seated emotional disturbances, beyond their narrow range of experience, would be difficult for them to accept. Their motivations for adoption are healthy, and they show an ability to work with the agency in providing for a child's needs. This is a warm, mature, relaxed couple, and both the child and the adoptive parents would benefit from a placement in this home.

The agency selected an older child for placement in the home and prepared the parents for this after having recruited, studied, and approvingly evaluated the couple.

The adoptive parents of course participated in a counterpart of the children's experience. The literature advises interview preparation of parents (23, 30, 43). In all cases the child to be placed was initially introduced to the parents by means of a presentation conference devoted to a verbal description of the child and his background. On occasion both the child's and the parents' adoption worker participated jointly in such a conference. Sometimes, however, the child's worker had briefed the parents' worker on the child and/or had provided the parents' worker with a written summary of the pertinent material.

The reaction to the verbal presentation was generally positive, and on the basis of this the agency arranged for a meeting between the child and the prospective parents. Once they had met the child, the parents were urged to discuss their reaction with each other, reflect on it, and let the agency know of their decision.

The literature suggests that the first reaction to the adoptive child is a sensitive indicator of the probable course of adoptive placement (5). The actual confrontation with the living reality of a child whom the applicants have to accept, or reject, as their own, supposedly mobilizes all elements of conflict in the parents' attitude toward adoption.

A very high percentage of parents in this study (82 per cent) were positive or positive ambivalent in their reaction to the child on presentation. They indicated little hesitancy in making the decision to accept the child. In a smaller number of cases there was some doubt and some delay on the part of the parents.

The following record excerpt is illustrative of the parents categorized as reacting positively to the presentation of the child.

They met the child in an enthusiastic, warm manner. They were friendly in their response to him but did not force themselves on him but rather let him take the lead in making and developing the association. However, they eagerly entered into his play activity and talked to him and asked questions in an interested manner. Occasionally, they would smile or laugh agreeably with some remark the child would make and they seemed to like him and be able to relate to him. Also, they seemed to be able to play at his level. From their first contact with him, they seemed to be favorably impressed, and it was also evident that they can relate to a child on a child's level. They engaged in activities which amuse and entertain a child of his age and seemed interested in pleasing him.

In one instance after a preplacement contact between child and adoptive parents during which it was definitely decided that the child would come live with them, the adoptive mother said she felt tired and happy. "I guess that's natural when you just had a child." Another mother shared with the worker the fact that she experienced cramps, which she described as similar to labor pains, when she met the prospective child on a preplacement visit.

The Postplacement Supervisory Period

After placement of the child in the home the agency retains guardianship of the child for a year. At the end of that time, if the placement appears to be going well and there seems no reason to anticipate difficulty, the actual legal transfer of guardianship takes place. A petition for adoption is acted on by the court. The adoptive parents become the legal, as well as the social and emotional, parents of the child, and the agency steps out of the picture. If, however, there appears to be some difficulty in the relationship between parents and child, or if there is reason to believe that this adoption placement is likely to be problematic, either the agency or the parents may ask for a continuation of the period of "trial" living and a postponement of the finalization of the adoption.

Most of these adoptions, 68 (75 per cent), were legally consummated within the minimum period, which suggests little hesitancy on the part of the adoptive parents or the agency. Ninety-three per cent of the group completed the process by 19 months. In a few instances delay was purely procedural—in 2 cases the family's lawyer had neglected to file the necessary papers; in another case the citizenship status of the child, born abroad, needed to be clarified. In only 4 (4.4 per cent) of the cases was it clear that delay in legal adoption was deliberate and arose from doubts of either the parents or the agency. In 4 other cases, while there was no delay in the legal completion of the adoption, the parent or the agency raised some question during the trial year about the advisability of delaying legal adoption.

The year between placement of the child and legal adoption affords the parents an opportunity to adjust to the role of adoptive parents. During this period the worker periodically visits the family. Parents tend to see these visits as supervisory in nature, a procedure to enable the agency to check on how the adoption is going. The agency tends to see these visits as educational, supportive, and therapeutic (26). These contacts enable the agency, through its worker, to help the adopters make the adjustments to parenthood, to help them with the problems they encounter, and to reassure them. From the agency's point of view such contacts help assure the success of the placement. For the agency, the parents, and the child, the trial period is a device which protects them from making a mistaken, hasty decision.

Since the adoption of older children is presumed to be more problematic the need for a close relationship between agency and family during the trial period is thought to be greater here than in other adoptive placements (10). Despite the great stress which the literature places on the importance of postplacement visits during the transitional period, they are actually quite infrequent. It is not likely that the limited number of contacts can actually effectively implement the therapeutic purposes which they supposedly serve. Among this group of parents agency visits averaged 3.6 per family per year.

This figure resembles visitation statistics from other studies. A study of 57 adoptive parents in Minnesota indicated that the median number of interviews per family per year was 3.83 (26,

p. 11). A highly professionalized private agency in a report on 37 adoptions indicated that the mean number of visits was 4.1 "office and home visits combined" (24, p. 584, Table 5).

The record included summaries of the social workers' contacts with the family between placement and legal adoption; 32 couples reported they adjusted readily. In 35 (38 per cent) of the cases parents adjusted with moderate difficulties. In 13 (14 per cent) of the cases they adjusted with considerable difficulty. In the latter cases there was some evidence of anxiety, depression, fatigue, disappointment, and resentment. In 59 (65 per cent) of the cases the primary emotional reaction following placement was one of happiness.

Results of a review of the record material regarding the older adoptive child's adjustment to the adoptive situation, the school, and the community were similar. Only 15 per cent of the children indicated "considerable difficulty" in adjusting.

One could anticipate a generally favorable adjustment on the part of both parents and children, since persistent difficulty would have been likely to endanger continuation of the placement and ultimate legal adoption. The generally favorable adjustment of the group during the transitional year is confirmed by a tabulation of the parents' expressed satisfaction and dissatisfaction as reported by the agency social workers. A total of 265 explicit satisfactions was reported for the group as against a total of 60 dissatisfactions—a ratio of 4 to 1.

We will reserve a discussion of the problems encountered by the parents in adjusting to the adoption for a later chapter, which reviews this subject as it appeared in our follow-up interviews.

While formal contact between the agency and the adoptive parents terminates with legal adoption, the agency then expresses willingness to be consulted in the future. The record indicates that in only 7 (8 per cent) instances did parents actually contact the agency after the legal adoption for help with a problem in the adoption. Twenty (22 per cent) other couples contacted the agency, but for the purpose of adopting an additional child.

_____ About half and half
_____ More dissatisfying than satisfying
_____ Extremely dissatisfying.

The distribution of responses for both the mothers and the fathers appears in Table VI.

Table VI   Parents' Choice of Level of Satisfaction in Overall Adoptive Experience

Level of Satisfaction	Adoptive Mother Number	Per Cent	Adoptive Father Number	Per cent
Extremely satisfying	53	58	57	63
More satisfying than dissatisfying	21	23	12	13
About half and half	7	8	5	6
More dissatisfying than satisfying	4	4	4	4
Extremely dissatisfying	2	2	1	1
Not answered	4	4	12	13
Totals	91	100	91	100

The parents were, in principle, free to choose any of the statements; yet one might postulate some social restraint as influencing the responses in a positive direction. Lower ranking responses might be interpreted as rejection of the child or as confessing failure as a parent. Self-protection or defensiveness might thus displace the rankings upward so that the response pattern may not reflect parents' true feelings.

We, therefore, asked the interviewer and each of the typescript readers to complete the same scale. The interviewer's ranking was based on her evaluation of total parent satisfaction as perceived in the interview; for the typescript readers, it was based on their perceptions of total parent satisfaction as reflected in the typescript of the interview. We computed a mean score for each of these 4 rankings—3 readers plus one interviewer. In 56 cases (61 per cent) the mean score computed was identical with the parents' ranking; 28 cases (31 per cent) had a one step difference; 7 cases (8 per cent), a two step difference. In each case where there was a 2 step difference the mean interviewer-reader ranking was lower than that of the parents. In 25 instances of a single step difference the mean interviewer ranking was lower, in 3 cases it was higher, than the parents' ranking. In general, then, there was substantial agreement between the parents and the interviewers-readers. Differences suggested that the parents were more optimistic than the independent observers.

A high level of agreement between parents and interviewers-readers might have been expected since the social workers based their judgment on what the parents offered in the interview. The workers are trained, however, to recognize discrepancies, distortions, and defensiveness in the parents' presentation and to draw inferences from them. This kind of evaluation of interview content led to a judgment different from that of the parents in 39 per cent of the cases, as noted above.

From these rankings we computed a final composite judgment of the mother's ranking, father's ranking, and the mean ranking derived from interviewers and readers. This gives greater weight to the parents' evaluation of the experience but still permits the corrective of the supposedly more objective judgments made by the interviewers and typescript readers.

The composite rankings are presented in Table VII.

Table VII   Parents', Interviewers', and Typescript Readers' Composite Score of Level of Adoptive Parents' Satisfaction in Overall Adoptive Experience

Level of Satisfaction	Number	Per Cent
Extremely satisfying	54	59
More satisfying than dissatisfying	17	19
About half and half	8	9
More dissatisfying than satisfying	9	10
Extremely dissatisfying	3	3
Totals	91	100

The composite ranking of parents' level of satisfaction correlated highly with the ratio of satisfaction-dissatisfaction scores
($r = .89$, $p < .001$). Where a ratio in favor of satisfaction was
3:1, or higher, we invariably found that the composite ranking
was in the "extremely satisfied" or "more satisfied than dissatisfied" range. Where the ratio was closer to 1:1, the overall
ranking of satisfaction fell in the half-and-half range. Any ratio
which indicated a greater number of dissatisfactions than satisfactions experienced invariably meant that the composite score
on overall satisfaction fell in the lower levels. Both measures
relate to similar material and use substantially the same content
in arriving at different kinds of answers to similar questions.

The two different kinds of criteria give us very similar outcome data: the composite ranking criterion indicates 78 per
cent of the adoptions as successful, 13 per cent unsuccessful,
and 9 per cent that might be regarded as intermediate. The
ratio of satisfactions to dissatisfactions criterion indicates 73 per
cent of the adoptions successful, 18 per cent unsuccessful, and 9
per cent intermediate. Success rates for the composite ranking
criterion run between a low of 78 per cent and a high of 87
per cent depending on whether one includes the intermediate
group in this category. Using the same procedure with the
satisfaction-dissatisfaction ratio criterion gives a range of success of 73 to 82 per cent. Related to the question of success is
the fact that only 2 of the 91 children placed had been removed from the home after adoption.

Comparison with Other Adoptive Outcome Studies

One needs some perspective in order to determine whether or
not this result is comparatively good. We need to know something about adoption outcome generally. Table VIII summarizes adoptive outcome studies so far available. We have included in it only studies in which definite information was
presented on sources of data, measures used for determining
outcome and a statistical statement of outcome (2, pp. 208–12,

Table VIII Adoptive Outcome Studies

Study and Date	Size of Study Group and Lapse of Time between Placement and Study	Outcome		Data Used for Follow-up Assessment	Auspices
		Number and Percentages	Outcome Criteria for Categorization		
Van Theis (1924)	235 (adults) 12–18 years after placement	207 (88.1%) 28 (11.9%)	"capable" "incapable"	Interviews with adoptive children, adoptive parents, and "other persons" by project interviewer	Agency
Morrison (1950)	24 (children) 10–17 years after placement	18 (75%) 6 (25%)	"getting along satisfactorily" "unsatisfactory adjustment"	Interviews with adoptive parents by agency workers	Agency
Brenner (1951)	50 (families) median of 4.4 years after placement	26 (52%) 18 (36%) 6 (12%)	"successful" "fairly successful" "unsuccessful"	Observation of children in home; interviews with adoptive mothers by agency workers; psychological tests of children	Agency

Study	Sample	Number (%)	Rating	Source of data	Type
Neiden (1951)	138 (adults) 15–20 years after placement	35 (25%) 62 (45%) 29 (21%) 12 (9%)	"very good" "good" "indifferent" "bad"	Records and interviews with adoptive parents by ag. soc. workers (?)	Agency
Armatruda (1951)	100 (children) at time of placement	76 (76%) 16 (16%) 8 (8%)	"good" "questionable" "poor"	Agency study of adoptive home; study of child by Yale development clinic	Agency
	100 (children) at time of placement	46 (46%) 26 (26%) 28 (28%)	"good" "questionable" "poor"	Agency study of adoptive home; study of child by Yale development clinic	Independent
Fairweather (1952)	18 (children) 3–4 years after placement	18 (100%)	"good"	Interviews with adoptive mothers by ag. workers; psych. tests of children	Agency
Edwards (1954)	79 (children) 5 years after placement	69 (87%) 9 (12%) 1 (1%)	"very happy" "some problems" "serious problem"	Information not available	Agency

Table VIII (continued)

Study and Date	Size of Study Group and Lapse of Time between Placement and Study	Outcome Number and Percentages	Outcome Criteria for Categorization	Data Used for Follow-up Assessment	Auspices
National Assn. for Mental Health, England (estimated 1954)	163 (children) minimum of 2 years after placement	142 (87.1%) 21 (12.9%)	"satisfactory" "unsatisfactory"	agency records	Agency
Davis-Dauck 1955	396 (children) 1 year after placement	371 (93.7%) 25 (6.3%)	not removed removed	Agency records records	Agency
Fradkin-Krugman (1956)	37 (children) during first year after placement	27 (73%) 6 (16%) 4 (11%)	"good" "intermediate" "poor"	On-going contact with parents during first year of supervision; tests of infant	Agency
Witmer et al. (1963)	484 (children) most 9 years after placement	324 (67%) 39 (8%) 121 (25%)	"excellent to fair" "not definitely unsatisfactory" "definitely unsatisfactory"	Interviews with parents and teachers by project interviewers; psychological tests of children	Independent

Lawder et al. (1966)	200 (children) (3–10 years after placement)	"superior" and "good"	127	Interviews with adoptive families	Agency
		"fair"	53		
		"low"	20		
McWhinnie (1967)	52 (adults) (16–66 years after placement)	"good" and "fairly good" "adjustment in all areas"	21	Interviews with adoptive children as adults	Independent
		"reasonable adjustment in some fundamental areas"	21		
		"adjustment poor in many areas"	10		
Ripple (1968)	160 (children) 9–10 years after placement	"within the normal range"	75 (47%)	Agency records; interviews with father, mother, child	Agency
		"some problems in adjustment"	47 (29%)		
		"serious emotional or behavior problems"	38 (24%)		

Table VIII (continued)

Summary—Recapitulation of Adoptive Outcome Studies

Outcome	Number	Per Cent
unequivocally successful	1,644	74
"not definitely unsatisfactory"	264	11
"fairly successful"		
"indifferent"		
"questionable"		
"some problems"		
"intermediate"		
"unsatisfactory"	328	15
"poor" "low"		
"problematic"		
"unsuccessful"		
"incapable"		
Total	2,236	100

8, 15, pp. 20–21, 19, pp. 3–8, 21, pp. 3–8, 23, pp. 577–90, 43, 51, 59, pp. 7–9 and 12–13, 61, 63, pp. 91–95, 69, pp. 479–96, 80, 91). Adhering to these criteria, we have not included follow-up studies such as those by Shaw (76) and Lynch (50). On such criteria, inclusion of the Edwards (19) study might be regarded as dubious. The study by Armatruda (12), although frequently quoted as such is not, strictly speaking, an outcome study, since assessment was made at the time of placement.

We have not included in the summarization follow-up studies of groups of children who presented special problems in adoption, such as the studies by Nordlie and Reed (64), Rathbun (67), Graham (28), or Welter (88) on foreign-born children placed for adoption in the United States (these studies, of more than ordinarily difficult placements, show a high percentage of "successes"). We have not included in the summarization a number of unpublished master's theses on adoption follow-up undertaken in schools of social work or the published summaries of such theses (62, pp. 44–45).

Comparisons can only be made in gross terms, since the studies differ from each other in many crucial ways—in terms of the criteria used in rating "success," in the rigor with which the criteria were applied, in the completeness with which data was collected, in methods of data collection, and in content of data collected.

For the total of 2,236 adoptions whose outcome was the subject of one study or another, success rates vary from 74 to 85 per cent depending on whether one included in the success group the intermediate category. Some 15 per cent were definitely unsuccessful. The present study outcome is very similar in terms of failure rate. On the composite level of satisfaction criterion, 13 per cent of our cases are rated definitely unsuccessful. Using the ratio of satisfactions to dissatisfactions criterion 18 per cent can be rated definitely unsuccessful. The range of successful cases is 78 to 87 per cent using the composite level of satisfaction criterion and 73 to 82 per cent using the ratio of satisfactions to dissatisfactions criterion. The middle group

Table IX Comparison Outcomes of This Study and Others

Outcome Selected—Previous Studies	Outcome—Present Study (Composite Score—Level of Parents' Satisfaction)			Number	Per cent	Outcome—Present Study (Ratio Satisfaction-Dissatisfaction)	Number	Per Cent
	Number	Per Cent						
unequivocally successful	1,644	74	extremely satisfying more satisfying than dissatisfying	71	78	2:1 or better	67	73
"fairly successful" "indifferent" "questionable" "intermediate"	264	11	about half and half	8	9	1:1	8	9
"unsatisfactory" "unsuccessful" "poor" "incapable"	328	15	more dissatisfying than satisfying extremely dissatisfying	12	13	1:2 or worse	16	18
Totals	2,236	100		91	100		91	100

of "fairly successful" cases is smaller for our study than it is for the totals derived from summarizing all the other adoptive outcome studies.

Table IX recapitulates the outcome of the present study for each of the two different criteria of success employed as compared with the overall combined results of the other studies.

Whatever differences there are between the successful adoptions of older children and that of the other adoptive studies tabulated here, they are not statistically significant. These, then, are the facts as far as we can ascertain them. The rest is a matter of judgment. Studies included in these tables for comparison with results of our group of older adoptees were, for the most part, studies of children placed for adoption in infancy.

Since the adoption of older children is regarded as a high risk, a placement that inherently presents greater problems for participants than the adoptive populations included in the summarizing tabulation, we might justifiably expect that our group would show a lower rate of success. It seems somewhat surprising, in the judgment of the author, that the difference does not appear greater. With the greater insults to psyche suffered by this group of adoptees during childhood, the social and emotional deprivation sustained over long periods of time, and the experience of placement and replacement while living with foster families in which they were only tenuously integrated, one might have anticipated a greater difference in success rates between this group of children and those placed for adoption in early infancy, for the latter knew only one family, one home, and one set of generally accepting parents throughout childhood.

Some Additional Confirmation of Outcome Statistics

The responses to two of the specific questions asked near the end of the interview confirm, once again, the parents' satisfaction in the adoptive experience. The first of these specific questions asked: "If you had a close friend who was seriously considering adopting a child between the ages of six and eleven what would you tell your friend?" The question was designed to permit the parents to share negative feelings indirectly by discussing their experience in a neutral context.

In 44 per cent of the cases the answer was a "positive," which means that "they strongly advised the friend to go ahead and this was said with no hesitation and with conviction." An additional 24 per cent of the parents responded in a manner which was regarded as "positive ambivalent," that is, they "advised the friend to go ahead but said this with some reservation, some conditional statements." Only 7 per cent of the parents "strongly advised against this and gave such advice without reservation and with conviction."

The most frequent response recommended adoption with conviction.

"I would say, well, go ahead."

"Uh huh. I would say go ahead and do it. If they don't have any more problems than we did it will be fine."

"Well, we would certainly say go ahead if that's what you wonder."

"I'd tell them there's nothing wrong with it."

"I'd tell them by all means—go ahead."

"I would not discourage them. I think it's a wonderful experience."

"I would recommend that they do it."

"If it could work out as well with them as it did with us I would say go ahead and do it."

The positive ambivalent group would recommend that the "friend" adopt, but suggest that he be prepared for problems, that it is a difficult, albeit rewarding experience. They recommend caution, and thoughtful consideration before going ahead. Some added that if the "friend" were younger than they were when their own child was placed with them they would recommend adopting an infant—that such a child was likely to present fewer problems.

MOTHER: I would tell. . . .
FATHER: This would depend in part on the friend's age. . . .
INTERVIEWER: Yes, well let's say it was about . . . somewhat the same age as you were.
MOTHER: As we were when we adopted [child] . . . ?
INTERVIEWER: Uh huh.
MOTHER: Well, I would certainly recommend it, wouldn't you?
FATHER: Yeah, I'd tell 'em they'd have some periods of great anxiety and uh . . . great heartache . . . as part of it.
MOTHER: Uh huh.
FATHER: . . . but I would tell them further that these are the things that go with bringing up children.

MOTHER: I think it would be a most rewarding experience . . . but it definitely is a hard job . . . this is nothing that you would say, "Oh, just go ahead and do it" . . . this is a hard job . . . not that you just work at it. . . . No, but I mean that you will have difficulties . . . yes, it really takes a dedication.

MOTHER: I would tell them there was . . . to think it over, and that it was a big problem that they're gonna have to face. It's more than I had realized, but I wouldn't tell them not to, but I would want 'em to be aware of what they were facing.
FATHER: I think the social workers downtown tried to tell us this, oh, it didn't sink in . . . you just can't. . . .
MOTHER: Yeah, but you just don't. . . . It doesn't sink in. . . .
FATHER: No, you can't realize what this is, until of course you've adopted a child and have her living with you.

And a few would discourage the friend from going ahead with the adoption.

MOTHER: No.
INTERVIEWER: No, um hmm.
MOTHER: They're just asking for heartbreak.

INTERVIEWER: *Asking for heartbreak?*

MOTHER: *I don't care how much information you get. A child over six has his patterns too thoroughly formed. Because children that have had such poor backgrounds as [child] are gonna have a awful problem. I . . . a person has a terrific amount of patience and has, oh, I don't know . . . I don't know what it would take. But I think it's almost impossible . . . to stand it sometimes.*

The second of the specific questions asked toward the end of the interview to elicit the parents' reaction to the adoptive experience was: "Looking back on the whole thing, and based on your adoptive experience, if you knew at the beginning what you know now would you do it again?" The question is poorly phrased and is somewhat directive since it terminates with an alternative already posited. Its format can be satisfied by a simple yes or no answer which in itself would yield only limited productive return. Nevertheless, the question leaves the parent relatively free to accept or reject the adoptive experience. Once again the largest percentage of the parents (67 per cent) responded without hesitation and with conviction that they would do it over again, the same way. Some 12 per cent were unequivocal in their assertion that, knowing then what they know now, they would *not* be willing to relive the experience.

The positive answers were generally short, clear, and emphatic: "Oh, most certainly"; "Sure"; "Absolutely"; "Very definitely"; "Oh, yes"; "Yeah, yeah, that's for sure"; "Oh, I'd jump at it"; "Very much so."

MOTHER: *Oh, yeah, sure I would do it again, quicker though. I don't think we ever felt discouraged about [child] have we, honey? You just can't help but love that kid. I guess he doesn't do nothing wrong? [laughing]. It isn't just because I'm blind you know. I do think some times you get blind, uh, and I feel that a lot of parents do get blind. But I remember our social worker telling us he used to always try and look at his children like a stranger would. And he said not to let your emotions rule you. I used to watch that.*

MOTHER: . . . but as far as adopting the boys, or adopting older children, I wouldn't change that.

FATHER: No.

MOTHER: I mean we have no regrets at all that we did adopt an older child. I think we would have done this before and not waited until we'd been married for ten years, but I would still have adopted older ones.

A few were plainly negative.

I would never now take a child over five or six, I wouldn't. Their ways are formed.

No, no. He was like a knife . . . stuck right into me . . . night and day . . . the concern and the worry . . . and the feeling. . . .

MOTHER: Going through what I have gone through? I've been screamed at, I've been yelled at, I've had things thrown at me, I've had a lot of heartaches, and I think that if I would have known then what I know now, I don't think that I would ever have gone through adopting an older child.

In general, then, these results reflect and support the criteria of outcome regarding levels of parent satisfaction in the experience and the ratio of satisfactions to dissatisfactions; they indicate that, for a large percentage of these parents, the experience was satisfying. With the developmental experiences of these children presented in Chapter 3, and their ages when placed for adoption, the results may seem somewhat surprising. Actually, to the adoptive parent group itself the favorableness of outcome was equally surprising. Fully 22 per cent of the group (20 couples) volunteered that it had worked out better than they had anticipated, that they had expected problems which never arose, difficulties which never developed.

FATHER: Well, uh, overall they gave us to understand that problems that adopted children . . . especially those that had . . .

were a few years old . . . might have lots of problems. . . . And
as I said, I anticipated those problems. And I think it was fine of
them to make you aware of what the problems could be! And of
course we got these youngsters and we didn't have these troubles
. . . [all laugh].

MOTHER: It was just a real pleasant surprise.

Satisfactions versus Dissatisfactions: Parent Response Forms

In Chapter 2, we noted that the parents were asked to complete
a response form at the end of the interview. One section
consisted of incomplete sentences, and the parents were asked
to complete them in any way they thought appropriate. The
incomplete sentence, if completed rapidly and without too
much deliberation, may elicit the more private reactions of the
parent without his being entirely aware of the feelings he is
sharing. Consistent with the rest of the data, the responses are
heavily weighted in the direction of satisfaction. Responses
from individual parents follow the interview material—satisfied
parents offer responses indicating satisfaction, dissatisfied parents respond negatively.

These parents write that "Our family

. . . has become a more complete and happy unit because of
the adoption of [the child]."
. . . is, by and large, a happy, contented one."
. . . is happier since we have had [the child]."
. . . is more complete now—for so long we were alone and it
seems now our house was awfully quiet at the time."
. . . has profited by having [the child]. I don't think that just
two people make up a 'family.' "

The responses to the stub "Being an adoptive father
(mother)" also reflect the satisfaction of most of the parents in

the experience. Thus they say that "Being an adoptive father (mother)

   . . . is the best thing that ever happened to me."
   . . . kind of makes me feel proud."
   . . . is a wonderful and rewarding experience that makes your life complete."
   . . . has given me the joy, pride, and responsibility of bringing up children."
   . . . has made me a happier family man."
   . . . keeps me extremely busy, and I like every minute of it."
   . . . is a wonderful experience, sometimes sad, sometimes happy, but mostly satisfying."

Adoptive parents who, according to our outcome criteria, had the lowest levels of satisfaction contributed 83 per cent of the comments categorized as neutral or dissatisfying in response to sentence stubs "Our family," "An adoptive family," and "Being an adoptive father (mother)."

These parents said that "Our family

   . . . life has been a disappointment."
   . . . has not been a completely satisfying experience."
   . . . has been under tension most of the time."
   . . . could be happier if the children were more cooperative."

They note that "An adoptive family

   . . . has more problems than the original parents."
   . . . has problems others do not have."

And that "Being an adoptive father (mother)

. . . hasn't been all the joy I expected it would be."

. . . is harder than being a natural mother, especially of older children."

. . . I feel I am a failure."

. . . is taking on a heartache."

The completions collected on two additional sentence stubs further substantiate the generally favorable response of these parents toward the adoption of older children. These were stubs "As an adoptive parent I wish I had . . ." and "As an adoptive parent I wish I had not . . ." Responses overlapped but were sufficiently varied to require separate categories. In response to the first sentence stub the largest single category of response was "I wish I had adopted sooner." Forty-five parents (25 per cent) gave this response. An additional 33 (18 per cent) answered that they wished they had adopted more. In response to the second stub 49 parents (26 per cent) said that they wished they had not waited so long to adopt children. This was the largest single response category to this stub.

Some of the responses regarding delay might be interpreted as implied dissatisfaction with adoption of older children, or an interpretation that if the parents had not waited so long, or if they had not been made to wait so long because of the agency's delay in processing their application, they might have been able to get these children when they were younger, and/or they might have been able to adopt younger children.

The negative sentence stub "As an adoptive parent I wish I had not . . ." prompted some expression of self-dissatisfaction in the respondents' approach to parenting, particularly concern regarding their response to the child.

Parents said they "Wished they had not

. . . taken every little thing so serious that the kids did in regard to what it was going to do to them as they got older."

. . . worried about the little things that in the long run seem to work out for themselves."
. . . scolded so much and so often."

However, the fact that here, too, the largest single category of responses indicated that the parents wished that they "had not waited so long" suggests satisfaction in the adoptive experience.

The response to these sentence stubs, as was true with regard to previous incomplete sentences, substantiated the negative views of adoption on the part of parents with lower levels of satisfaction.

These parents wrote that they "Wished that they had

. . . looked into the background of the child more."
. . . more knowledge of the child first."
. . . spent some time finding out more about his background."

And conversely "They wished they had not

. . . rushed into the adoption in such a short time."
. . . been so eager."

The Satisfactions and Dissatisfactions Experienced by the Adoptive Parents

We noted above that 3 typescript readers identified specific items of satisfaction and dissatisfaction either explicitly or implicitly expressed by the parents in the interviews. We also noted that of a total of 1,927 items identified by all of the typescript readers 90 per cent of the items were independently identified by at least 2 different typescript readers. The 1,740 items that were identified by at least 2 different typescript readers were tabulated. The 187 items identified by no more than one reader were discarded.

Table X   Listing of Specific Parental Satisfactions and Dissatisfactions in the Adoptive Experience; in Descending Order of Frequency

Satisfactions	Number of Families Expressing This Satisfaction
The Child Himself: Personality, temperament, disposition	79
Relationship to Extended Family: Accepts and is accepted	71
Parent-Child Relationship: Companionship for and with parent	69
The Job of Parenthood: To watch and help a child grow and develop	63
The Job of Parenthood: An interest and purpose in life	62
The Child's Achievements: Contribution to household maintenance, chores	55
The Adoptive Situation: Success in helping child accept, adjust to adoptive status	52
Child's Achievements: Accepts and is accepted by friends	51
Parent-Child Relationship: Affectional responses between child-parent	51
The Adoptive Situation: Resolution of a problem of accepting adoptive child	51
Child's Achievement: Prestigious hobbies, interests, skills	50
The Job of Parenthood: Successful handling of day-to-day problems	50
Parent-Child Relationships: Obedient to, respect for parents	49
Child's Achievements: Attitude toward school, school progress	49
Child's Achievements: Sex—appropriate activity	41
The Child Himself: Physical attractiveness	38
The Child Himself: Good physical health	36
Parent-Child Relationship: Identifies with parents	36
Sibling-Sibling Relationship: Shares, not competitive	36
Child's Achievements: Satisfactory routines, eating, cleanliness, etc.	32

Satisfactions	Number of Families Expressing This Satisfaction
Child's Achievements: Membership participation in community groups	31
Child's Achievements: Handles allowance well	28
The Job of Parenthood: Increased appreciation of simple things in life	27
Sibling-Sibling Relationship: Companionship for and with siblings	27
The Job of Parenthood: Satisfaction in homemaking skills, ability to feed, clothe, care for the child	23
Physical-Social Environment: Providing adequate housing	23
The Adoptive Situation: Success in handling child's divided loyalties	21
The Adoptive Situation: Success in handling child's questions about adoption	21
The Job of Parenthood: Setting a good example for child	21
Parent-Child Relationship: Child's pride in parents	20
Parent-Child Relationship: Child confides in parents	20
The Child Himself: Emotional health	19
The Adoptive Situation: Community evaluation of adoptive status	18
Relationship to Extended Family: Considerate, polite, companionable	14
Parent-Child Relationship: Sympathetic understanding when parents troubled	13
The Job of Parenthood: A link to the future	9
The Job of Parenthood: Satisfaction in ability to consider needs of child	9
Miscellaneous	12
Subtotal	1,388

Table X (continued)

Dissatisfactions	Number of Families Expressing This Dissatisfaction
Child's Achievement: Attitude toward school, school progress	55
The Child Himself: Personality, temperament, disposition	38
The Child Himself: Emotional health	31
The Job of Parenthood: Self-reproach, self-doubt about competence as parent	24
Sibling-Sibling relationship: Jealous of, conflict with	19
Parent-Child Relationship: Lack of affectional response	17
Parent-Child Relationship: Does not confide	17
Parent-Child Relationship: Disobedient, disrespectful	17
Child's Achievement: Socially shy, isolated, unliked	17
The Adoptive Situation: Difficulty in accepting child	15
The Adoptive Situation: Problems in handling divided loyalties	13
The Adoptive Situation: Difficulty in getting child to adjust to, accept adoptive situation	13
Child's Achievements: Problems around routines, eating, cleanliness, etc.	11
Child's Achievements: Lack of contribution to household maintenance, chores	11
The Job of Parenthood: Anxiety about child's getting into trouble, discrediting family	11
Parent-Child Relationship: Lack of companionship for and with parent	11
Parent-Child Relationship: Rejects, derogates parent	10
Parent-Child Relationship: Rejects identification with parent	9
Child's Achievement: Handles allowance poorly	9
Child's Achievement: Lack of prestigious interests, hobbies and skills	9
Miscellaneous	4
Subtotal	352
Total satisfactions and dissatisfactions	1,740

The particular items of satisfactions-dissatisfactions which were checked in descending order of frequency are presented in Table X.

Table XI lists the general categories of parent satisfaction and dissatisfaction.

The child's achievements are the principal source of both satisfaction and dissatisfaction. This may be because such behavior is observable and easily describable. In addition to this,

Table XI   Satisfactions and Dissatisfactions in the Adoptive Experience by General Categories

Category of Expressed Satisfaction-Dissatisfaction	Satisfactions		Dissatisfactions	
	Number	Per Cent	Number	Per Cent
The Child's Achievements	339	25	106	30
The Job of Parenthood	269	19	35	10
Parent-Child Relationship	265	19	72	20
The Child Himself	172	12	63	19
The Adoptive Situation	170	12	43	12
Relationship to Extended Family	85	6	6	1.5
Sibling-Sibling Relationship	53	4	21	6
The Physical-Social Environment:				
Home and Community	35	3	6	1.5
Totals	1,388	100	352	100

however, we tend to measure our success and failure in effectively implementing our roles as parents in terms of the end product: the child's performance and achievements. The general concern of the culture with achievement as a measure of a man's worth would tend to suggest primary concern with what the child can do and secondary concern with what the child is. Concern with achievement is also concern with the community's perception of the family. The child represents the family in the wider community. What he does, and how he does it, is capable of reflecting credit or discredit on the parents. The child in school is tested against, and compared with, other children in standard situations. All parents are sensitive to such comparisons but this may be particularly true for adoptive parents who received the child as a result of community action and who might, therefore, feel more accountable to the community for the outcome.

Parent-child relationship factors are a second principal source of both satisfactions and dissatisfactions. An unsatisfactory situation is more apt to be related to the child himself: his personality, temperament, disposition, and emotional health; where the situation is satisfactory this is more likely to be related to the job of parenthood. The adoptive situation itself is both a potent source of satisfaction and dissatisfaction. If it goes well, that is if the parents find that they themselves can resolve the problems of adoptive status and help the child to resolve such problems, such problem solving is a source of satisfaction. If they fail to do this, the fact of failure is a source of dissatisfaction in itself but, further, the unresolved problems occasion difficulty and dissatisfaction.

So much for a numerical overview of the major findings regarding the adoptive parents' level of satisfaction-dissatisfactions. Excerpts from the interviews give what numerically expressed information cannot conceivably give: a sense of the feeling these parents have for these children; the good and the bad feelings, the accepting and rejecting feelings. This is data in itself, perhaps the most important and significant kind. Through excerpts from the typescript we will attempt to present a more graphic picture of the satisfactions and dissatisfactions experienced by these parents in these adoptions.

Satisfactions-Dissatisfactions: The Child Himself

The child himself, his personality, and attributes frequently produced both satisfactions and dissatisfactions for the parents. Parents characterized the children in ways which indicated the pleasure they derived from them. Different parents talked of different children as being "sensitive," "compassionate," "lovable," "effervescent," "friendly," "thoughtful," "tolerant," "a bubbler," "likable," "gentle," "cooperative," and "appreciative." They said, "He's a good boy—like gold," "he has a good way with hens," "she's a friendly little kid," "he has a kind heart," "she's an all-round good kid," "a fun kid," "a bundle of laughs," "a good guy," "sloppy as heck but an awfully sweet girl," "just a real easy child," and "he's nice to have around."

On the other hand, parents spoke of their children as being "irresponsible," "infantile," "destructive," "bullying," "sharptongued," "hurtful," "demanding," "dependent," "uncommunicative," "defiant," "stubborn," and "mistrustful." They complained that a child "had limited enthusiasms," "doesn't show happy feelings," "is hard to live with," "is walled off," "is the tired blood type," "the plow-horse kind of kid," or "is easy to anger."

A child's personality—his temperament and character dispositions—is thus a source of satisfaction for parents.

MOTHER: *Yes, well, that's the way he is . . . he's very responsible and he makes friends. . . . He has a good personality. It maybe sounds like we're bragging or somethin' but that's the way he is. . . . but you don't find children that way all the time . . . but he is, he fits in well at anything . . . he's in 4-H, and I've never had any problems with him in anything that he's joined or anyplace that he goes . . . he's always well, so he just happens to be that kind of child . . . just lucky, he's easy and . . . he takes things in his stride as a matter of fact . . . sure, he doesn't like discipline like any other kid. If he could get away without it, he'd be the first guy to say that [laughing]. But he accepts it, sure, he's that good natured.*

MOTHER: *And he's fun to have around . . . he really is terrific. "Hi, there, kiddy, how's my girl?" You know . . . and crazy little things like that . . . and then he'll wipe dishes with me and he's a good egg . . . he really is . . . of course, you can hear me bubbling over . . . the proud parent. . . . But, I mean, he really* is . . . and we can be very, very grateful that he has turned out as he has, and I think that he has a lot of good qualities that are important. . . .

FATHER: Oh . . . [sigh] . . . when you . . . see her with other kids and so forth, you're very happy that she's your daughter. . . . There's a group in our neighborhood that puts on plays . . . we have a drama group . . . she volunteered to be the official baby-sitter for them while they were practicing and while they had it. This was . . . evening after evening and Saturday after Saturday . . . with no compensation . . . this was a volunteer thing, and things like this make you proud that she's yours . . . and when other people compare her with other children and she stands out a little bit above in appearance and poise . . . her big asset is her poise and her ability to meet people and . . . she impresses people, adults, very nicely because she doesn't say anything.

And sometimes the parents' satisfaction in the child's personality is briefly but pointedly stated.

MOTHER: Well, I enjoy having her. She's a lot of company for one thing. And she's a good kid and we don't have to tell her twice.

MOTHER: He's good company . . . [pause] and he saves mother's feet a lot . . . [laughs].

Very often the good qualities and bad qualities, the sources of satisfaction and disssatisfaction in the child himself, are presented side by side.

MOTHER: Well, [child] has many fine qualities . . . she's a happy child, which is real important . . . I think . . . she gets along very well with people, with her own age group, with older folks, with little children . . . she's a regular little mother, she can take over a group of little folks and just mother the whole group . . . or she can be with a group of her own and be the life of the party and lots of fun. . . . She has a very nice personality. And she's an excellent student, she does very good work in school and certainly is a girl we enjoy having around home, so there are . . . she's just a good all-around girl. . . .

INTERVIEWER: What are her shortcomings?

MOTHER: Well, that to me, you have to have a few things . . . she gets a little pouty once in a while . . . and, oh, a little sassy once in a while, and I'll really have to just scold her and sit down and tell her . . . and once in a while her table manners aren't what they should be, and I scold her for that . . . and she resents this quite a bit.

FATHER: She has many good qualities—love for small children, older people . . . her sensitivity. This is one of her beautiful characteristics, extremely sensitive child, has a . . . seems to have a boundless feeling for the other fellow. If either of us are sad, she's sad. . . . On the other hand, she has a very short attention span, extremely short for an eleven-year-old, extremely short. I would say her attention span would be commensurate with what we normally associate with six- and seven-year-olds. And because of this short attention span it plays over into other parts of her life. She doesn't get her school work done. It doesn't bother her either. If she doesn't get it done today, why, it'll get done tomorrow. If it doesn't get done tomorrow, so what, you know. And then of course, she does have this tendency to be careless about her person. If her mother didn't watch her . . . she'd be dirty and smelly.

And there is pride and satisfaction in the physical appearance the child makes; this is another aspect of satisfaction in the child himself. Also satisfaction in having a child who is healthy is noted.

FATHER: You see him sometimes, you know, when he's just bubbling over with enthusiasm, and it gives you that good feeling inside . . . you know that. . . .

MOTHER: Um hmm. To know that he's happy. And you see him out on the water skis or something, and there's this beautiful body standing there on the water skis. And you think of this little kid that was just wandering around all alone. Then he gets dressed up on Sunday and looks so gorgeous.

FATHER: That's another thing that I've appreciated about him, of course, he's been real healthy. He's an outdoor boy . . . and I don't care if it's twenty below out he's outside . . . and, uh, golly, he just hasn't been sick, I think in the, well, how many years have we had him . . . ?
MOTHER: Four years.
FATHER: I think we paid. . . .
MOTHER: Four years this fall. . . .
FATHER: Oh, golly . . . we've paid less than ten dollars in medical . . . uh . . . [pause].
MOTHER: Yeah, he's a real healthy youngster [pause].

But for other parents the child's personality—the child himself—is a source of deeply felt dissatisfaction.

MOTHER: Oh, I'm worried about her. She doesn't . . . from the very beginning . . . she, uh, well, she doesn't care about anyone . . . really. I can't get her to actually care. About anyone. That's the only thing, the cat, that she really cares about. Her brother doesn't mean too much to her. We don't mean too much to her. She likes, uh, maybe she even loves us, but . . . she's very impulsive. She wants what she wants when she wants it . . . and she's very selfish. And she's been that way from the very beginning. And I can't break her of that. She said she's always looking for her own happiness and I told her, "You can't be happy yourself unless you make others happy." But it doesn't go through to her. Like our minister said, she knows her religion beautifully but refuses to practice it. It's a case of living on a surface with her. You can't get close to her. I think she's been shifted so much that really she's afraid to actually love anything.

MOTHER: He wouldn't, uh, listen to any rules and regulations . . . you couldn't tell him anything. Explain to him and he understood it and yet he'd do just the opposite. He was always damaging things, I mean . . . throwing stones or . . . breaking windows and . . . destructing, going out to other peoples' yards and pulling their flowers out or . . . just nasty little things like that.

Sometimes the expression of dissatisfaction with a child's personality is more specific and centered on a single trait very annoying to the parent:

MOTHER: She doesn't have too much patience, does she? [to husband] Do you think you would say that?
FATHER: She doesn't have any.

MOTHER: Well, what gets me down most about her is . . . [pause] . . . well, I would say her untidiness . . . that's what aggravates me more than anything . . . and I'm not a particularly straight person . . . I'm not too fussy in the house but her room . . . [sighs] . . . it looks like a hurricane struck it most of the time . . . and now we can ask her to straighten it up and she will . . . she'll go upstairs and straighten it out . . . the next time you look at it . . . it will be in the same condition again . . . and that includes the bathroom.

MOTHER: He's a hard child to live with, and he's a hard child to give love to . . . let's just put it this way . . . he doesn't demand any love because he doesn't give any love . . . he doesn't even know how to kiss a person. . . .

Satisfactions-Dissatisfactions: The Child's Achievements

Another major source of satisfaction and dissatisfaction lies with the child's achievements: in school, in his social relationships, in his ability and willingness to contribute to household maintenance and management, in prestigious hobbies and interests, memberships in community organizations, and appropriate sex-linked activities.

The parents speak with pride of the child's achievements in school and in community organizations and artistic and athletic accomplishments.

MOTHER: [Child] is growing into such a lovely young lady, ah, she's very good in her schoolwork . . . at school this last year, after school was closed, I went in to see the superintendent . . . and to line up her school subjects for this next year . . . and he said, "Well, we'll have to check and see what grades she had in her different aptitude tests and everything," and he said, "Oh, my, she had about an 11.2 average which is junior second year." And he said she can have . . . she can take anything she wants . . . she's been an excellent student . . . and now in eighth grade they're able to take the first year of French so [child] was one of those upper ten in eighth grade that completed her first year of French, so she goes into her second-year French as a freshman in high school . . . which is real wonderful, I think, she has been a very good student.

MOTHER: She gets very good grades and she has learned to play the violin and what other instrument was it that she played, a tonette?

FATHER: Tootaphone, flutaphone.

MOTHER: Tootaphone, or something like that.

FATHER: Well, they're not very shattering events, same way with the others but, uh, each little achievement you like to see and . . . and encourage 'em. Even though the . . . they may squawk to beat the dickens on an instrument, but as long as they can pick out the melody of what they're trying to play, why—that's an achievement.

MOTHER: Well, he's done all right, he's . . . he's, what should I say . . . he's not really dumb, but he's the type of kid that dreams when he's doing his homework. He likes to draw airplanes or ships or . . . you know what I mean, he doesn't concentrate.

FATHER: Real good artist. [Mother laughs.] Likes to draw. He had about five or six exhibitions here in the fair. He's done sculpturing and things like that, real good. He takes a terrific interest in that stuff.

MOTHER: I laugh when he brings home his papers from school; he might have a seventy on the paper, but on the back of his paper he has the most beautiful looking ships [laughs].

FATHER: Yeah, he'll draw anything.

MOTHER: I think he'll be all right. He's come a long way. But he was very, very slow when we got him. He couldn't read. Of course, he's still not a very good reader. We help him with that . . . but in all his subjects he was weak. Of course, he didn't have anybody to take an interest in him.

FATHER: He is very deeply interested in fishing and, of course, having a spinning rod now, as he got for last Christmas, I believe . . . we got him . . . we got him a good reel and rod. . . .

MOTHER: And that is the third one he's had.

FATHER: . . . and also the ah . . . tackle box and he likes to go fishing . . . he goes out to this boy friend's and yesterday, it amazed me. I was in the kitchen and he was out in the back yard, practicing. Casting. He puts on a heavy sinker and casts and he called, "Hey, Dad." I went to the door and went out on the porch and he says, "Look, I found out . . . I learned a couple new ways to cast." He had his, ah, sports magazine out there on the lawn . . . and had been reading, and then he showed me . . . he says, "The bow and arrow cast," and he showed me. "Here's the grasshopper cast . . ." and the what else was it . . . and he showed me . . . and he had amazed me with, ah, fact . . . ah . . . that he became so adept at handling the rod and reel . . . all by himself.

MOTHER: And he chose the Peace Corps which I think is an interesting thing . . . for his speech subject . . . to talk about . . . they had a question and answer period, I was really quite proud of him, that this little guy who couldn't talk too well was not afraid to get up there and do that where all these other children. . . . But I was very happy about that, and because he's always been shy, you know, and reticent about forging ahead and getting to know people . . . that I was quite impressed that he would even say, "We have a question and answer period." You know, "I'm here to answer whatever questions you have." So . . . [laughing] that kind of tickled me . . . that he did it.

MOTHER: I think the last one . . . not the last piano recital as much as the first one. She just really surprised us. Because I thought she'd be kind of nervous about playing, you know, and getting up in front but . . . there are I don't know how many

students and [child] walked right up there and she stood up and
"I'm going to play the uh. . . ." Oh, what was it she played, the
bass viola, oh, I don't know. I can't remember the piece any
more. And she sat down and started playing and, oh, I was so
nervous for her, you know, I was going like this, and I was looking at her, and she played that thing just right off the bat.

MOTHER: We've had a number of fossil-hunting trips out
at _____ County . . . and [child] is very good at spotting fos-
sils . . . and this makes her feel important . . . she can really
spot them. And I remember one of our first trips . . . this is
something she has talked about again and again. And the
teacher told me about this too that [child] told her . . . there
was one fossil that was especially . . . especially odd . . . especially nice, the one that she found up there . . . she can spot them
. . . the rest of us walk along, looking and digging . . . which
made her real proud. And there was this one that she got . . .
and, uh, I looked at that, and I was so thrilled. I just picked her
up, and I squeezed her and I hugged her . . . and I shook her
. . . and everything else, and she has talked about that again and
again . . . how it was when Mommy hugged me and hugged me
and hugged me . . . because I found that fossil which was good,
see.

The parents detail the satisfactions derived from the child's
willingness to cooperate in work around the home.

MOTHER: . . . there isn't a thing you tell him to do, he wouldn't
do. . . . I don't care what it is. . . . No matter what you
tell that kid to do he would do it and he would never say a
word. . . .
FATHER: He's just a good kid, now I'm just telling you [laughs].
MOTHER: Tell him to do something, why . . . once in a while he
might . . . he might . . . say he don't wanna, but he'd go and do
it . . . [laughs]. Might not be too agreeable . . . but he never
wouldn't do it . . . wouldn't have to tell him twice.

FATHER: Yeah. Now he got where he can drive the truck you know
. . . and stuff like that . . . [long pause]. You never have to

worry about feed . . . like yesterday he thought the feed was a little low . . . and him and [brother], go get the truck out . . . and we got a new pickup . . . and they load it up and take it down here to the feed mill.

MOTHER: Grind it . . . and he was gone . . . he was in the fields . . . did it themselves.

MOTHER: You know what [child] did, uh—I think since he's been in second grade we've got thirty-five cows,—he gets up every morning and finds the cows. . . . And he'll lock the thirty-five head of cows up, and then he'd come in and he'd say, "can I make you coffee, can I do this for you?" And he's never, he's doing something all the time. Oh, that boy, I . . . someone said, well, maybe he's holding in. But [child] isn't holding anything in, you can see he never loses his temper. He doesn't get mad, he doesn't get angry about anything. He hasn't got nothing to hold in.

There is, obversely, dissatisfaction with the child's lack of achievement, his failures in school, his lack of ability to make friends, or in his choice of friends who are unacceptable to the parents.

MOTHER: She just couldn't learn her numbers, she couldn't, she couldn't learn anything, it seemed like she had a mental block there. You could go so far, and then you couldn't get any more into her, and different times we tried to teach her at home and, uh, she just, she just couldn't get it. Then we'd lose our patience, I would, and my husband would try it with her and he'd, of course, he wouldn't lose his patience but he would just say he couldn't teach her . . . we tried . . . we tried different things, like she wanted to be a tap dancer, to do dancing, well, we took her to dancing lessons, three or four times . . . we enrolled her, and after the third or fourth time she didn't want to go any more. She just couldn't learn which was her right foot and which was her left foot, and things like that. That was enough to do it. So we quit it. We thought rather than push her into something she can't do . . . then she took up a musical instrument. She wanted to do that real bad. And, uh, it seems like when she got in with the group to try . . . couldn't do anything . . . wouldn't practice . . . she hated the thing, you know. So she dropped that. And then, as far as her singing voice, she loves to sing but she's got the flattest voice you ever saw, or heard. First we found about it was, we knew her voice wasn't too good but she just loved to sing, so we thought we'd just let her sing. And she went to choir at church and then we found out the director was telling her not to sing, just move her lips, see? Well, finally he told her not to come back to choir any more because she was throwing everybody off with her flat voice. There really isn't anything she is good at. Well, she can make different things out of these boxes, today it's so easy. And she likes to try all those new things, and I have different things on hand here and she'll take it off a recipe. Well, at different times she's tried it. She made a dish for me about a week or so ago and she, ah, something her girl friend told her about, and anyway she put it in the oven and when she come to serve it—somehow she didn't put no liquid on it . . . and it was real dry [laugh]. I felt so sorry for her and she says, "Just another flop." [Laughs.] But we ate it. And I said, "It wasn't bad, it could have been a little bit juicier but it wasn't bad," but then she resolved she'd never try it again.

FATHER: And this past year in school he flunked in all his grades and he's not stupid . . . he's not stupid. He's carefree. Anything goes . . . today or tomorrow, it doesn't make any difference. . . . He doesn't like school. . . . He doesn't like to study. . . . He doesn't like to work . . . period. He's got a lazy streak in him.

MOTHER: He was just, uh, a little bully. He'd always pick somebody to have for a friend who was in the low category.
FATHER: Below himself. . . .
MOTHER: Below himself . . . he couldn't make up with the better kids, wherever he went to school he'd find, I mean, whatever class he'd go to he'd always pick out the bad guys.

MOTHER: He just needs his social problems to be ironed out. He just can't make friends . . . he has nobody . . . not any real buddy. Now at the Boy Scout meeting, he came home and I said, did you pass your test, and they were passing physical fitness. He said no, and I said why not. He said, well, none of the kids would hold my feet down, and they were doing sit-ups. None of the kids will pair off with him. And he isn't the kind that . . . he'll push a kid to get . . . to make friends . . . you know go up and push him on the back. . . . He doesn't know how to approach to make friends. . . .

Satisfaction-Dissatisfaction: The Parent-Child Relationship

A separate group of satisfactions is concerned with the relationship between child and parent: the pleasure in companionship between child and parents, in confidences shared, in mutual interests, the reciprocal giving and receiving of affectional responses, the respect for, appreciation of, and identification with the parent by the child, and the acceptance of the parents' disciplinary efforts, as well as the sympathetic responses of the child when the parent is troubled or ill—all these are sources of satisfaction for the parent when experienced. The child's failure to reciprocate affection, his disrespect, derogation, and rejection of the parents are sources of dissatisfaction.

Parents need love, acceptance, and appreciation from the child just as the child needs them from the parents. The parents have satisfaction when the children are capable of, and willing to, demonstrate a good feeling for them, a feeling that they like the parents, that the parents are people of importance and significance to them.

FATHER: Yeah . . . one time she . . . well you had her down to the office in church . . . and she had typed out this . . . She made one for you, didn't she [to wife]?

MOTHER: Yeah . . . she made. . . .

FATHER: She made out this, uh, typed out this little note . . . on a piece of paper, one to each of us . . . on mine it had, "Dad, I love you . . . very much. . . ."

MOTHER: His was just like on mine . . . "I love you very much

. . . *love M _____ R _____ very, very much" in red.* . . .

FATHER: *Yeah.*

MOTHER: *The note has a picture of a little girl kissing* . . . *see she's all puckered up* [shows to Interviewer].

INTERVIEWER: *Oh, yes* . . . *presented it to you.*

FATHER: *At lunchtime. It kind of made me feel like a heel because I was* . . . *well, it was one of these days, you know, that you have every once in a while* . . . *that, uh, you're quite irritable* . . . *with work, and then you come home and you try to drop this* . . . *well, sort of cloak of irritability* . . . *at home* . . . *and you just don't quite succeed* . . . *and, uh, and she didn't help matters any, and then just about the time I was ready to grit my teeth and grab hold of the chair and hang on real tight then she, "Here Dad* . . ." *she gives me this paper, and I said, "I don't want that thing." I'm about ready to toss it away, and then* . . . *I get the hint I'm supposed to open it up, and there's this* . . . *this message, you know, you just kind of feel you've shrunk to about an inch tall, you know.*

MOTHER: *Oh, well, she* . . . [pause] *would, ah, I'd be sitting there* . . . *like, ah, reading* . . . *which isn't too often* . . . [laughs] *but, ah, but just trying to relax, and she'll come over and sit next to me* . . . *and she'll say to me* . . . [sigh] *"I'm so glad you're my momma." I think, oh, all those problems are nothing* . . . [laughs] *you know.*

MOTHER: *I do know that* . . . [child] *had never had very much mother love, and when we first got her I couldn't* . . . *put my arms around her very well, and you have to take it easy with children that age. You can't just grab 'em and hug 'em* . . . *you know. I was affectionate to her, and I'd kiss her on the cheek and* . . . *or something* . . . *gradually* . . . *I asked her if she knew that she had beautiful eyes, and she just looked at me, nobody had ever complimented her* . . . *nobody had ever told her that* . . . *she had lovely hair, and she did have pretty eyes* . . . *and she had a beautiful complexion. She had a cute little body, and I thought if I can work this up* . . . *and make her feel equal* . . . *and, ah, and so I, you know, she'd be standing near me* . . . *now he could tuck her in, and kiss her good night, but when*

I did, I had to be awfully careful 'cause she'd, ah, kind of, just kinda cringe a little bit. You know, she'd kiss me, but I could just . . . so finally, oh, dear, I think we had her over two weeks, and we were eating . . . so she came around and I put my arm around her. And I thought, well, I'm going to take a chance. And I just grabbed her and hugged her, and she just burst into tears. She cried and cried, and she hugged me and she cried, and I said, "What is the matter? Have I done something?" She said, "I never had a mommy love me before." Six years old. And that's why she was afraid of the hugging. Never had a mother. So we just have ideas that [child] got kind of kicked around because she has some scars, I mean we don't know where she got them, and she said, "Mommy, I never had a mommy hug me before." And from then on, did I get loved. It was heartbreaking. From a six-year-old child. And never had a mother love her before. I cried worse than she did. Oh!

FATHER: Shortly after he came, he came rushing over to my office, he was crying his heart out, he was afraid to call his mother, He had gone to the ten-cent store and had picked up a harmonica. Course that happens whether they're adopted or not, but that was our first moment of fear, you might say, but we handled that . . . by not too strict a lecture, but explaining to him and insisted that he go back to the store and tell the manager he was sorry.

MOTHER: Yes, but you know what he said to me afterward, the worst part of it was that he had hurt you so badly by doing that . . . he said, "I hurt my Dad."

MOTHER: There was one occasion that stands out in my memory . . . and I think it always will, I don't know if you remember this or not [to husband] but remember when I was working at ——— and you weren't feeling good, and you thought you were blacking out or something, or that you were having a heart attack or something, and he was home and he called me on the phone and he said, "Mother, there's something wrong with Daddy." And he was just all shook up, and I said, "Well, what's wrong?" and he said, "I don't know. Daddy's real sick, and I don't know what to do, and you'd better come right home."

*And he was just . . . oh, hysterical, you know. . . . So, I told
my boss, I don't know, there's something wrong . . . my husband came home from work and I don't know if he's had a
heart attack or what . . . 'cause I didn't know if [child] was just
overexcited you know . . . so I got home and he had . . . we
have, we each have a little crucifix in our bedrooms, and he went
to his room and got his little crucifix and [laughs] he put it on
the dresser upstairs, and he was praying . . . you know, and
Daddy was lying on the bed, remember? And he was just praying that nothing would happen to my husband and I say . . . I
think that's one of the most outstanding things that I'll never
forget. Yes, I was just all choked up.*

Satisfaction is derived from the companionship of children,
from the child's readiness to share his inner life with the
parents, and from his indication of respect for the parents and
willingness to accept parental discipline.

MOTHER: *Oh, we've had them out in Wyoming, Montana, Idaho,
they've really seen more than most kids their age. Ontario and
Quebec and we've had them up into Manitoba so far we couldn't
go any farther. And we had the advantage of the midnight sun.
I think that's the biggest thrill they'll ever have in their life.
Really, oh, I don't know, there's a lot . . . . They're good com-
panions and . . . they sure took ten years off our lives. I could
mean that both ways [laughs heartily]. I mean ten years younger
but it works both ways [everyone laughs].*

INTERVIEWER: *Well, it does work both ways.*

MOTHER: *Yes it does [laughter] but they took ten years off at times
too. I won't, I won't retract that statement a bit.*

FATHER: *I think they've been a lot of fun to be with, ah . . . .*

MOTHER: *[Interrupting] Well, they like to do the things we do.
They like outdoor life . . . there's nothing they like better than
to get out in the woods with the dog and away we go, and, ah,
we go up to _____ quite a lot, I don't know if you know where
that is, it's quite a mountain, and there's a river runs down in
the woods there, we love to go up there in the spring and, oh,
shove a great hunk of ice out and watch it swirl down through*

the rapids and, oh, so many little things they love to do. And,
ah, they just love outdoor life. And so do we. I don't know,
they're fun. They put a lot of joy in our lives and a lot of worry,
sure, but so what. Everybody has worries.

MOTHER: *I think that companionship of father and son is just*
wonderful because my husband was very much attached to his
father . . . and he lost his father just three years ago . . . when
his father died it hurt, you could tell . . . it was a little bit hard
on him . . . his father passed away in the spring, in April, I
believe, but he and his father had been deer hunting for—oh,
years, you see. So that fall, when it was deer season, we all just
hush-hushed about it . . . because we just didn't know what was
going to happen . . . and here he picks up [child] and says,
"H_____, you're old enough to go now," there . . . he fits
right in . . . . It just happened, but it was just perfect, and of
course, [child] was just thrilled to pieces . . . [laughs]. To this
day now his dad takes him on every hunting event he goes on
. . . [child] goes with him, and he has been going for two or
three years now . . . the two of them . . . they bought the dog
out there . . . the beagle . . . . That's theirs together.

MOTHER: *The times I really enjoyed were when . . . it's quiet . . .*
it's always been with me alone . . . when, you see, my husband's
in the office two to three nights a week . . . and then he's had
sometimes one and two nights of lodge . . . . So staying home
with him in the little times when he would tell me things . . .
that happened before [takes a breath] and things that he
liked . . . "Do you remember, Mother . . . do you remember
when we'd turn out all the lights, and we'd go around the
house . . . and look out every window . . . and see all the
things we could see . . ." The do you remember time . . .
when we talked. . . .

INTERVIEWER: *Those were the nice times.*

MOTHER: *Those were the times when I thought how nice it is to*
have him . . . and what a joy he is.

MOTHER: *Oh, she talks with me, when she's bothered about some-*
thing, she'll just talk for an hour, she has no problems talking. I

notice we have a lot of good conversations when I'm ironing. I suppose I'm available more then.

MOTHER: *She comes from school and just confides everything . . . she'll tell me everything . . . and just goes on . . . which is very different from our son . . . he would tell you some things but then there were things in school that he never bothered much about telling . . . and this I enjoy thoroughly . . . I love it. . . .*

INTERVIEWER: *This has been a big satisfaction to you.*

MOTHER: *Yes . . . because I just thoroughly enjoy sitting down and listening to her when she comes from school, and we learn all the things that were good and bad about the day and, you know, this is just real interesting to me. . . . and I enjoy it and so does [husband]. He will sit and enjoy listening to anything she has to tell us . . . about school or anything else, where she's been. . . .*

MOTHER: *Well, like this Girl Scout work . . . of course, that has been a part of me . . . and, ah, she is very proud to say that I'm their leader . . . but like she always says, "Mom thinks young" [laughs].*

Satisfaction and pride comes from the child's identification with the parent and manifesting it. One father put it succinctly when he said, "Anything that he didn't like that I ate, he ate."

MOTHER: *He has the same name as Dad, too. He is kind of proud of that . . . one day, ah, maybe this would be something . . . he made the remark, I don't recall just exactly what it was but I told him, "You know, J———, you sound just like Dad," and he said, "Well, I want to be like him, I want to imitate him." Imitate him . . . he said it himself . . . right out . . . so you can see that in the back of his mind, he has made an impression . . . this is the one I am going to be like . . . or want to be like . . . and he has taken on mannerisms like, ah, when he was little, you could see him walk behind his dad, and he sort of walked like him . . . he tried to sway or, ah, you could just see it. . . .*

FATHER: It's rubbing off a little bit, the nature of the child. You know, it's big strong daddy. His little sister made the remark that, what did she say, that [child] is sure getting to be. . . .

MOTHER: . . . just like Dad. She said he's just as big a carcass as Daddy.

FATHER: And he really has taken on my ways. Oh, fishing and swimming, I taught him to swim. You catch him every once in a while telling the other kids, "Well my dad did this," and it sure gives you a good feeling. . . .

FATHER: And I don't think that they could be any more . . . ah, like us, or take on our characteristics any more than if we had them for a longer period, say from a younger age. M_____ walks down the road and he looks just like me, and I walk down the road and I look just like my father [laughs]. Whether it's conscious or unconscious, I don't know, but, ah, you should see the two of us going down the road, you'd think we were father and son. . . .

MOTHER: . . . [the child] . . . has taken on many of my mannerisms. Fortunately, I'm not too feminine, I wouldn't want a boy to take on many of his mother's characteristics but he'll scold his younger brother, you know, and I'll see him talking [laughs], poking his finger and shaking it at him [still laughing], it doesn't take long, even with older children, for them to . . . I hear them use the expressions we use.

FATHER: She will tell people things, I know that the neighbors have told us things that she has said that we have done, she will . . . quote things that we have said . . . that while she wouldn't agree with us to our face, "Oh, this is ridiculous, this is silly." But she will go out and immediately quote the same thing to someone else. And she's, ah, many times she's told the women in the neighborhood things that my wife has said, or things . . . how to do things . . . that my wife would do . . . this way . . . but she wouldn't admit that my wife . . . could do anything. But, ah, underneath it all, she . . . seems to think the way we think.

Other parents, however, have not received affection from their adopted children. Instead of acceptance they have faced rejection, instead of respect they have experienced derogation, instead of being included in the inner life of the child they have been shut out.

MOTHER: *He just isn't affectionate. He isn't. He has never been an awfully affectionate child, the kind that will just come up and throw his arms around you or anything like that. Well, I could be affectionate, but he would not return it, maybe that's what I should say.*

FATHER: *Well, this is something that you have to learn, he didn't know how to give affection because he never had to give it back, you see.*

MOTHER: *But I just don't think it's his nature particularly either, because very seldom, in eight years, has he just impulsively come to give either of us any . . . kiss or hug or anything like that, it just isn't in him to do that. And we've accepted it, at first I kept waiting for it, and now I've decided it just isn't in him . . . so. . . .*

MOTHER: *You couldn't take [child] and put your hand on her; you couldn't put your arm around her and love her. She'd push you away, or a lot of times she would slap back at you. And I never could do anything that exactly pleased her, even to just fixing her hair. Well, she always knew somebody who can fix it better. Or if, at their birthday parties, someone would give the comment of how lucky you are that your mother can bake so well, these buns and things are delicious, right away she would comment, well, I know someone who can do better. That hurt; I'm a human being and I think a mother and father has a right to expect as much love in return as you give. I don't think that all this love should be a lopsided thing. We just can't sit and accept things all the time and take for granted and not want to give anything back in return. Haven't I the right, as a mother, to expect those things? Those are the things we expected when we adopted children. And I don't think we are unfair by expecting those things. I shouldn't have to have my sister's youngsters come here and sleep with me to have the feeling of it, should I? I have to do it.*

MOTHER: *I think, but, ah, I think one thing that's hard . . . for him is to accept me . . . to tell me everything . . . there's several*

times when I've come on him where . . . he's in . . . he's trou-
bled about something, and I try to encourage him to talk about
it but he doesn't let me in . . . he keeps things to himself and
shuts me out.

Where the parent-child relationship is positive, the perception of resemblance, of identification, is accepted and welcomed. Where the relationship is troubled, the imputation of
identification is rejected. It implies a dissatisfying accusation
against which the parent defends himself.

MOTHER: *I think that a hundred times a day probably I looked at*
her and would think, "Boy, this is what I'm like," because they
told us that they try to match personalities [laughs] . . . and I
just thought, "Boy, I certainly hope I'm not like that . . ."
[laughs] I don't know what kind of impression I gave the social
worker and the homefinder if that was the kind of person I was
. . . [laughs]. No, I wouldn't say that she was too much like me.

Satisfactions-Dissatisfactions: The Occupation of Parenthood

A parent finds special satisfactions in teaching a child, in providing for one, in helping him to grow physically and to develop socially and emotionally, in successfully coping with day-
to-day problems. There are satisfactions in meeting the child's
dependency needs and in setting a good example for him. It is a
job which provides continued interest and stimulation, gives
significance and meaning to life, and decreases self-centered-
ness. It humanizes the parent, helps him grow toward greater
maturity and understanding, and affords him common interests
with other parents.

FATHER: *I don't know, it seems like now . . . [pause] we're, ah . . .*
well, we got something to look forward to. . . . Before it was

just . . . from daylight to dark . . . the same thing every
day. . . . Now, by gosh. . . .

MOTHER: [Breaking in] . . . Now, it's not the same thing every day
[father laughs]. One week it's take 'em to bible school; the next
week it's 4-H, and the next week it's swimming lessons . . . we're
on the road all the time, now . . . [everybody laughs] so it's quite
a change. They've been warning us that when children get older,
you spend time on the road luggin' 'em around and boy . . . this
summer we've sure found it out, I mean . . . they seem to enjoy
it.

FATHER: Well, I know . . . the biggest change as far as help you
know . . . holy smokes, now I don't have to run . . . for every
little thing.

MOTHER: They're very good about helping, they're, ah. . . .

FATHER: Man, oh, man . . . they save me . . . oh, I'd say about
half of my running work. . . .

FATHER: Well, I get a big kick out of teaching him things, you
know. I think that's the biggest thing of it . . . and then
watching him grow up, you know, learning things on his own, I
think. . . . And, of course, you watch him develop, as you teach
him different things, and then they grow up. And then you'd be
surprised they . . . it gives you a lot of satisfaction when they
take ahold of something . . . you probably think you're not
getting any place and then all of a sudden . . . they just seem to
pick . . . catch on, you know. It takes so long. . . .

FATHER: They were so amazed . . . early in the morning about
3:30 . . . on this camping trip . . . I could see they were a little
bit chilled even though we had a fire going, sleeping on the
ground is a little bit chilling, and so they started to wake up and
get close up to the fire, and I said, "I'll make you a cup of hot
tea, you drink that, and then I'm going to make you some soup."
All we carried was one pie tin and cup . . . ah, the wonder of a
child, and they were just so amazed about certain things, and I
said, "Yes, I'll make you some soup." "Well, what kind of soup
can you make out here?" "Well, beef soup." All I had was some
bouillion cubes, but they had never seen anything like this. And,
ah, I made them this soup, and they thought that was terrific—

to make beef soup out here without having any beef with you, you know [laughs], and I think maybe I should have been a teacher because I enjoy showing them little things and . . . teaching them something. . . . To teach a child to do something . . . . Now [child] is learning to ride his bicycle . . . but he cannot ride it yet. Well, if you'd like to get on and, you know, show him how it's done, but you can show him, and show him, and show him, and still he has not been able to learn. Well, it's gonna be a great day for me, it'll be a great day for me when he does finally learn to ride that bicycle [laughs].

MOTHER: Well, you enjoy their feelings of accomplishment, I think. This is a big thing. When they accomplish something and are able to do it themselves . . . they're pretty proud . . . and you enjoy their accomplishment.

FATHER: They were so proud of being able to climb that rope because I couldn't do it. . . .

MOTHER: Anything that they can do that he can't do just tickles them. You know, they're so much more agile than he is . . . they can wrap their legs and arms and, ah, he [husband] had them sitting here fascinated one night 'cause he picked up his leg and tucked it behind his head. They didn't think Daddy could do anything like that, you know [hearty laugh] . . . turning himself into a pretzel and wondering if he'd get stuck . . . [laughs].

There is the satisfaction which comes from being able to act as an example and mentor for the child.

MOTHER: Oh, when we were shopping oh, two weeks ago, and every week I have to get a dozen oranges, my husband likes his orange for breakfast, so we go shopping twice a week, and this happened at the end of the week. Ah, no, this happened at the beginning of the week. I go shopping on Monday and Friday. So Monday we went shopping and he and I were picking out oranges and we were counting too fast. When I got home there was thirteen oranges in the bag. So I said to [child], "We made a mistake, we got 13 oranges for the price of 12." I said, "Next time we go shopping you remind me to take 11 the next time." "O.K." So we just dropped that. So the next time we went shopping I remembered it. And when we saw the pile of oranges, I remembered it . . . and there were no bags around so I just put the oranges in the basket. So when we came to the checkout I put them all on the checkout table, and the clerk naturally would count them, and she said, "There's only 11 here." And I said, "Well, last week when [child] and I were shopping, we were both counting and we made a mistake, we got 13. So I thought this week we'd take 11." And she looked at me and she said, "My, but you're honest." And [child] when we got outside in the car, he said to me, "Mother, you sure are honest." [laughs] He was impressed . . . so if you do these things in front of the children they will learn to do them too. I didn't do that to be so honest . . . I didn't take the 13 on purpose and there was no . . . I didn't have to take 11 the next time, you know, but it was a good thing to show off in front of him.

Satisfaction comes from being able to provide adequately for the child, to meet the physical needs of the child, and to help him grow.

MOTHER: Most of their things when they came were just rags and I, well, my heart just ached. Their underwear wasn't even whole. Their panties weren't whole at all, they were just rags. And I think one of the biggest thrills in my life was when I went down to the stores down here and bought them quite a few outfits and took them home and I told the girls, "Here's yours and here's yours," and they were just stunned! Weren't they? I mean we didn't overdo it, we just bought, oh, four or five dresses apiece, and our biggest problem was when the teacher had a fit with [child] because [child] was bound she was going to show everybody her new underwear, and she'd never had pretty underwear before. We just, Oh, you would have thought she'd committed a crime. I said, "Well, if you'd never had a pretty petticoat in your life wouldn't you want to show it?"

MOTHER: Well, she was a very little thing when we got her. And. . . .
FATHER: Forty-eight pounds.

MOTHER: When she ate and ate. . . . She filled out in a hurry but, uh. . . .

FATHER: Well, she weighed forty-eight pounds when we got her, and she weighs in the eighty pounds now.

MOTHER: Eighty-two. She grew over six inches . . . over six inches . . . almost seven. I don't know when I measured her.

MOTHER: You haven't seen our little boy! [laughter] When he came here he was a little shorter than I was, and I said, "Well, good, now I won't have to be the shortest one in the house," and he looked at me like, well, that's not gonna take long! [more laughter] It sure didn't. He's fifteen and, oh! he is just a big husky boy now. Well, he is just big. Big shoulders and great big ankles.

FATHER: Husky. Heavier than I am, I know that [laughs]. He's got broad shoulders and more. . . .

There is satisfaction in coping with the usual problems of child rearing.

MOTHER: I see that that's my job, to be here . . . get the kids up . . . give 'em a good breakfast . . . get 'em off to school . . . be here when they come home. . . . And it's a job I enjoy doing.

MOTHER: He would do it so quietly, this demanding attention. He'd come to me, and in a soft voice he'd talk and tell me . . . "see what I did out here at the boat . . . I stepped on a stone and there was a little scratch. . . ." You know, but it was done so kinda quietly that, I didn't make a lot of it . . . another thing I thought I wouldn't do was scold him for it . . . in front of the other children a lot, then it would kind of make it so evident. But then again, I would just let it go and say, "Well, that is too bad. But that's okay, that's gonna be all right." Then he . . . he'd just kind of forget about it. . . . But . . . I asked the teacher about that when we had the conference, "Yes," she said, "if he has had something that's happened on the playground, you know, he always comes and tells me about it." So you see, he . . . he liked to have adults interested in him. Another thing . . . he will interrupt once in a while like . . . like if someone is visiting he'll come up to me, "Momma," and he'll interrupt. Oh, it's taken

quite a while to work that out . . . but then some of it's kinda
normal . . . so I don't make a lot of it. But, uh, I try to answer
him quickly, and he goes on his way . . . but it's—often times
it's very insignificant. . . . He just wanted to tell me something
outdoors, uh, that doesn't matter to these people at all. But
everyone likes [child]. [Emphatically] Very well-liked. So many
will say, "My goodness he's a nice little boy." Yes . . . he likes a
little attention.

FATHER: Just a general satisfaction in watching a couple of real nice
kids grow up and maybe helping. And having a family of your
own.

MOTHER: It's a . . . there's problems, just like we had our own
when we were growing up. I mean, it isn't all easy . . . there's
very nice things to come out of it, and also many problems. I
think the nicest part is to see them develop, and just last year
they really have shown a lot of love and expression, and anger,
which I don't think they were allowed to show too much, and I
think it's wonderful to be able to explode and be able to say, "I'm
sorry and let's forget it, let's make up." These things they weren't
allowed to do, I don't think. They are able to do that now
because we helped them . . . to develop this . . . helped them to
express themselves more.

MOTHER: Oh, they were awfully hard learning boys . . . I don't
think, uh, from home I don't think . . . that they had any
pushing at all, as far as schooling goes. . . . They were so
hard-learning. They didn't want to read . . . that was . . . you
know, right from the start . . . oh, I had to do some talking, well,
I helped them along . . . with their studies in the country school.
Till they really got into it . . . that they knew that they should
do it, you know. You know, they were awfully far back when they
. . . but they surely learned a lot since . . . they were here . . .
in the few years. . . . And they never used to read . . . well, we
bought 'em the Popular Science and the Popular Mechanics; they
like to putter around with things like that . . . now they're
starting so they'll take the daily newspaper and look at it and read
things over and. . . .

MOTHER: *He didn't want to go to school. . . . Well, I'll tell you . . . I'll tell you the truth . . . I couldn't even get his shoes and stockings on him. . . . When he had to go to school . . . I had called up my sisters . . . this was . . . three mornings in a row . . . to help me . . . to get him dressed . . . I felt so sorry for him . . . I cried myself. But you couldn't . . . back out here . . . he'd be way . . . way behind . . . I couldn't give in . . . I . . . I . . . I . . . just couldn't give in . . . we . . . didn't spank him . . . we just . . . and of course he kicked and talked . . . and. . . .*

FATHER: We forced him to go. . . .

MOTHER: *. . . and we just had to get him to go or . . . I . . . and then I took him to school . . . I had to carry him out of the car, oh, I felt so sorry for him . . . and he . . . wouldn't get on the bus . . . well, I wasn't there in the evening. So he had to come home on the bus . . . and pretty soon . . . he . . . and then the bus driver, you know, that drove the bus . . . who was our friend . . . so to make it taste good he came out a couple of evenings you know . . . to get him used to this bus driver . . . and I told the bus driver . . . you know the situation. . . . I think he's a little shy, see . . . about getting in with the driver and a bunch of kids . . . but he came out . . . and, oh, I think it was—how many days was that? . . . and I think it must have been two . . . I think it was. . . .*

FATHER: Yeah . . . two weeks.

MOTHER: *. . . approximately two weeks before we got him on the bus in the morning . . . but then he had to . . . he didn't miss a day that year . . . his first grade . . . he didn't miss a day his second grade. His third grade he had mumps . . . two . . . about two weeks . . . and the fourth grade he had flu . . . two days . . . but he had gone practically every day to school. So he . . . has done real well.*

INTERVIEWER: Yes . . . once he started, he really kept on with it.

MOTHER: *Yeah . . . oh, yeah . . . he goes . . . he don't want to miss school now . . . after he got going.*

There is satisfaction in having another human being depend on you and feeling confident that you can meet the child's needs.

MOTHER: Well, I'll tell you, like for instance, you bake something . . . I baked a batch of cookies yesterday [child] came in and he said, "Boy, Mom, those are good cookies. . . ." and then he says, "They should be, you made 'em . . . everything you make is good." . . . and then they'll say something about it and the girl will say, "Yeah, we make the same thing in school but when you make it it's a lot better." You know, it gives you a feeling of—you're really doing something. And in the morning . . . [Pause] . . .

INTERVIEWER: It's the little things. . . .

MOTHER: It's the little things, sure, but they add up . . . the little, every day. . . . They'll come in "Hi, Mom, Hi, Dad," and they'll probably say it six times before they finally get settled in a chair and settled in a place, you know. . . . Course he is more that way than the girl . . . he'll say good night maybe three times before he finally gets up to bed, where she'll say it once and that's enough, see? . . . but that's the idea of a little bit of insecurity again . . . he wants to know that we're here, and it's just good to know he's depending on you. . . .

MOTHER: Well . . . we have found that our life without any child . . . you know . . . if we hadn't of gotten him . . . well, I think that you're selfish if you don't have a child . . . I think so . . . and it's kinda hard to go around living among your friends, too, and they all talk about their children, and you set there and listen but you don't have anything to say. . . . You can't get in on the conversation if you're without children . . . well, I think all the way around it's just wonderful . . . it helps us . . . and it certainly helps him . . . to have someone he knows loves him, you know . . . and it gives you a good feeling to know that somebody cares for you, you know . . . somebody depends on you a little bit . . . and it's different that way . . . it helps that way. . . .

INTERVIEWER: So it gives the parents a lot too.

MOTHER: I think so . . . I would certainly encourage anybody to adopt a child . . . if they don't have any of their own.

MOTHER: Well, as you know, I think every woman knowingly or unknowingly has a mother instinct and having something small or more or less helpless, whether they be our boys' age or younger, to love and help and care for is the most natural thing in the world and, ah, this is the biggest joy I've had . . . this being able to love and take care of these helpless little people. And they're pretty helpless [hearty laughter] . . . sometimes I think they're hopeless! [laughing].

Also, satisfactions in parenthood come from being able to see the world through the eyes of a child, in reliving one's own childhood experiences, in growing toward a greater maturity as a result of responding to parents' responsibilities.

MOTHER: Oh, it makes me feel good when she comes in that door and says, "Hi, Mom, what's doin'?" Just that. I don't know that there's anything special . . . it's just everyday things. . . . Everything has been . . . our holidays, Christmas, has been more meaningful with him. Our vacation trips perhaps have been more meaningful because we've seen things we wouldn't have otherwise . . . we've come down quite a bit. . . .

INTERVIEWER: To the child's level . . . ?

MOTHER: Yes . . . enjoying the simple things of life rather than . . . don't you think?

FATHER: Probably . . . yeah. . . .

MOTHER: For everyday living. I don't think there's any . . . of course Mother's Day and Father's Day mean more, naturally . . . but . . . in other words, just everyday living is just a real satisfaction.

FATHER: The prayers that she makes up spontaneously at the supper table. Or before she goes to bed. The things she says. . . . They . . . are the happiest. . . .

FATHER: Well, we collect things, collect all kinds of things.

MOTHER: Now we have birds' eggs. We love nature, we love outdoor things, so we're either collecting rocks or collecting shells along the road, or we'll go to a place where we can hunt so and so . . . birds' eggs or bird feathers, or . . . but they're things around us. Ordinarily, I think, without children, maybe we would've passed by. I think that is one thing she has, one of the biggest *things that she has brought to us is love of the simple things that you don't get in adult life. I think that a child . . . gets excited about things like that, and the excitement spreads to the parents.*

MOTHER: Oh . . . it's having the responsibility . . . of . . . of, uh, molding a young life so that they're a satisfaction to themselves and the people that they'll love. . . . It, uh . . . [pause] is, of course, a tremendous responsibility . . . and therefore quite a satisfaction when you see any progress that seems to you to be in the right direction.

FATHER: Well, this is one thing about having a child, too, you . . . you learn from the child, I mean, the child teaches you . . . as well as you teaching the child . . . I know I've, uh, have learned to control my temper a good deal with her around. . . . Of course, I control it more since I've been married, too, than when I was single but, uh, well I don't know whether I'll get the right word I'm after . . . well, one thing that they can teach you is not to hold a grudge . . . I mean . . . I . . . a child can and that used to be one of my faults . . . well, if she was naughty and deserved it . . . you could give her a spanking—five minutes later . . . she's in your arms with her arms just tight around your neck and [laughs] almost chokes you . . . and then there's . . . there's no indication by her actions that she has gotten a spanking, and as far as anyone would be concerned she's never gotten a spanking, and I mean she doesn't show that . . . she doesn't hold that against you [pause]. . . .

INTERVIEWER: So you felt that this was a . . . good for your character? [laughs]

FATHER: Yes . . . [laughs] . . . real good.

FATHER: Having children in the home even, ah, even a rock becomes very significant and . . . because children see all these things and . . . and in such a different way from adults . . . because adults become so . . . stilted and unenthusiastic . . . that, ah, you're at an opportunity to, well, live another life, so to speak. This to me . . . is very important . . . and I think it's very important to my wife too.

MOTHER: And in some ways . . . we hope to . . . maybe . . . [sigh] maybe be able to guide them a little bit . . . I mean, our purpose is to guide them . . . but in many ways . . . I . . . I think, ah . . . you don't guide them completely . . . I think there are certain patterns that are a part of them and . . . you can help them recognize these things. . . .

FATHER: Well, as I said before . . . the chances . . . of having another life, experiencing things anew . . . sharing their enthusiasm and . . . well, altering your . . . what has become stilted outlook on life . . . let's say. . . .

MOTHER: Seeing it more through their eyes. . . .

FATHER: Yeah.

FATHER: Some of our friends have mentioned the change that has taken place in us, a different attitude towards life, and I, well, I'm not as much aware of it, I can see what they mean. Like this business of being happier, or more contented . . . I know I'm finding more meaning in life. We were out Wednesday night . . . took the boys out to the river fishing—camping and fishing, it was the first time we had been out just on a fishing trip without sleeping bags and tents and things like that . . . and it's interesting to see their reactions as I think back [laughs] . . . it's very much the reaction I had the first time I spent the night in the woods . . . with the bears and the deer and everything around and listening and looking at . . . you can live your life over again in them, really, your childhood.

FATHER: When you have children I really think you do think of the feelings of other people a lot quicker. I think before that you're really kind of self-centered. You just think of your own wants. I don't know. I don't think we really were that self-centered. We both come from such a large family. I come from a family of fourteen and [wife] comes from a family of eleven. And I just doubt very much that you could be self-centered after coming from a family like that. But it's different 'cuz they're not your responsibility, and when you're parents of course they are your responsibility . . . they are, uh, your own.

Parenthood gives meaning and significance to life; it provides a sanctioned, acceptable, satisfying goal and focus for an individual's activities.

MOTHER: *Oh, it makes your life full. I know of so many, eh, people our age who are lost. They are, uh, looking for new things . . . and new places to go and places to eat . . . and they either can't afford it or can't get out. But, uh, it's kinda pathetic when you see them. They just don't have an interest. Always looking for something to do . . . and with having a child there is always something to do.*

MOTHER: *Well, I wouldn't part with them for anything. . . . There are days when I'd just as soon give them away, wouldn't even ask . . . put a price on them . . . but I know . . . one . . . day when these friends of ours . . . invited them over to stay overnight . . . and we had looked forward to this for some time . . . because we were going to have an evening to ourselves. . . . And we wanted to go out and eat . . . were going to visit some friends of ours . . . and this was all so nice. . . . And we came home to an empty house . . . and we went upstairs and there were two empty beds, and it was . . . just the most empty feeling. . . .*

FATHER: *Mmmhmm [pause] . . . to know that they weren't there. Sort of . . . they really, ah, we've all become a part of each other . . . in, ah . . . in a pretty short time.*

MOTHER: *Well, with a child you know . . . you're not . . . you're worrying about other things besides yourself . . . well, it was—if we wanted to go we went . . . and if we wanted to stay home we stayed home . . . and if we wanted to go dancing we went dancing . . . and we had no problems . . . we didn't have to worry about anybody . . . but still there was something lacking, 'cause you weren't working toward anything. . . . I mean, like I say, it's like one of these questions, what your goals are, you have none . . . but when the child came . . . you have something then . . . otherwise, what is the sense of killing yourself if you're only going to work for the two of you? We were both working . . . and he'd bring home a paycheck, and I'd bring home a paycheck, and we'd go out . . . that was it, we had nobody else to worry about . . . well, it's just work, work, you know? . . . you have no purpose. . . .*

MOTHER: *Well [sigh] it was always just the two of us, no matter where . . . it was always just two of us . . . and you get kind of*

. . . [pause] well, I shouldn't say bored with [laughing] each other . . . either, I don't know [laughing] it just kinda seemed there was nothing to do. . . .

INTERVIEWER: Yes.

MOTHER: You know . . . there was just nothing to keep you busy . . . it was just. . . . You couldn't share anything . . . with anybody . . . it was just the two of us . . . and then . . . when ah . . . we had them coming . . . oh, then it . . . seemed so good to hear feet running in and out . . . and . . . let you have something, ah . . . to put your affection on I guess. . . . I don't know . . . how to, ah, explain it either . . . but it was just, ah, it seemed like when they . . . had been there for . . . well, even after the first few times . . . they were there for a visit . . . then they went away . . . gee . . . if I'd pick up an old doll that she left behind . . . you know . . . it kinda hurts you in. . . . I think your affection just rips a little deeper then. . . .

MOTHER: Well, what fun would it be for us to go on the sandbar and sit there in that dirty old sand, looking at the hills if [child] wasn't there puddling around in the water. I mean that's a simple example. Or what good our pasture, or what good would those horses be in there, if we didn't have him to ride them and have all the others . . . you know, he's always got kids out here . . . if he didn't have these other kids down there to ride them and so on. Or what good would Christmas be if you couldn't anticipate his happiness Christmas morning? That type of thing. Or even. . . .

FATHER: It's nice to have somebody else around you can live with real easy, you know.

INTERVIEWER: It's nice to have somebody else around. . . .

MOTHER: You know, isn't that funny, how you just don't stop and think of these things, do you? You just take them all for granted.

FATHER: Well, without kids, what else'd be the sense of you working?

INTERVIEWER: I see. Uh huh.

FATHER: To me, uh, sure my folks had a lot of kids and never thought nothing, but yet you build your farm, and you work like a darn fool, and well, first we had the eighty acres and then we had that seventy we bought to it. That was before we had the kids wasn't it?

MOTHER: Um hmm.

FATHER: Of course, who are we going to leave it to? I suppose the state would take it or the county gladly. So you might as well have some kids and share some of that with 'em. For her maybe that was different. When she got old she wanted somebody to look after her!

MOTHER: [Laughing] I did! You think that's what I thought?

FATHER: Sure.

MOTHER: Well, you know that isn't such a funny idea. I have my dad with me now. He's been with me for, uh, four years. It's good to have kids for when you're old.

MOTHER: What's nice about having him? Well, I don't know . . . having him around . . . talking to him. . . . He lived on a farm and he's interesting. . . .

FATHER: Of course, there's a lot of things, I don't think you can explain it. Really . . . it's hard to explain . . . I mean it's just nice knowing he's around. And you'd be surprised when he goes off to Scout camp. . . .

MOTHER: That's when I miss him. When he's here you take him for granted, you know, but when he was gone, I thought, gee, I'd hate to live all alone again, you know, without [child].

INTERVIEWER: Yes. Then you know you have something.

MOTHER: Yes . . . and, uh, I thought, my . . . he is a lot of work . . . when he's here . . . 'cause I didn't have anything to do [laughs] in comparison you know. I thought I surely wouldn't want to be without him though . . . and they depend on you for so many things . . . maybe that's the nice part of it. . . . You know, they ask you about things, and. . . .

FATHER: Well, you feel you're doing something useful, too, I mean actually. . . .

MOTHER: That's what I think. . . .

FATHER: I mean, after all, you're helping the kid a lot . . . I mean, maybe he don't appreciate . . . maybe you don't even appreciate what you're doing, but I think in the long run . . . you do. I mean, it's like anything else, take these hospitals that help different children and stuff, sure. I mean to a lot of people it doesn't mean anything . . . but to the people that are doing it, it means a lot.

And the job of being a parent has responsibilities that are a source of considerable satisfaction if they can be met successfully. Particular difficulties and problems are thus cited not as dissatisfactions but as satisfactions. They provide opportunity for feelings of accomplishment.

MOTHER: *The oldest one, we had a little problem with. She was blind in one eye when we got her. The foster parents knew it but they said . . . she said she didn't want to wear glasses and they never had her eyes fitted. And so, ah, she also had buck teeth, and so she really went through quite a lot for several years, with that bad eye with patches and treatment and this and that. I took her over to _____ and we really had quite a fight on our hands to save it, but now without her glasses even, 20–30 or 20–40 vision. . . . We're real proud of that fact. . . .*

FATHER: *20–20 with glasses. . . .*

MOTHER: *20–20 with glasses, and she wasn't using the left eye at all, it was just dormant. And, ah, she just had her braces taken off last year. But [child] never complained. That was the thing I couldn't get over. As little as she was, six years old, with this black patch on her eye, and all that, and you know how cruel children can be, she never complained, she just never made one objection to it. To all the things we were doing to her. We explained to her that, ah, what we were doing, of course, and she knew, and she never, well, when she got her first pair of glasses, [laughs] well, we were sitting at the dinner table and her glasses came in the mail, and she put 'em on and she looked up at me, "Where'd you get all the wrinkles, Mother?" [hearty laughter]. She'd never seen them before because she didn't have glasses on. And then she looked all around the room, "Oh, it looks just like a Christmas tree." She'd never distinguished the color I guess. But it was so cute, "Where'd you get all those wrinkles, Mother?" And she was wonderful. She just adjusted so fast.*

FATHER: *I think there are satisfactions, too. The things we mentioned are things that came about because of neglect . . . were not normal, because someone had definitely neglected to carry out what I felt was their responsibility. And to be able to do something about the problems . . . that was a satisfaction.*

MOTHER: *What are the satisfactions in having* [child]. . . . **Oh, now you've got us going. Oh!** *You just said did we mind the extra responsibility? I think that's one of the joys of having children. Is that feeling that you're needed. And it's a challenge. I'm so, ah, so proud of the way that, for instance, what we've done, I know and so does* [husband] . . . *and those girls, from everything . . . that those girls would be walking the streets. We know it from the things they've said, that they'd both be walking the streets. And to see them growing into fine young ladies, we hope, and, ah, I don't know, I think it's a feeling of achievement and companionship and being, being needed. Doing something worthwhile and being needed and wanted.*

FATHER: *It's been a lot of fun actually.*

MOTHER: *It's a lot of worry, but I don't think that kills . . . nobody ever died of it. Of worry and, ah, oh, I don't know, it's just too big to explain. You can't . . . you can't. . . .*

Satisfactions come from feeling included in membership as a parent with other parents and in sharing a common significant experience. It increases understanding of the problems of parent-child relationships and increases empathy with other parents.

MOTHER: [Breathless] *Oh, I don't know* . . . [voice trembling] . . . *when we first went to adopt . . . the child . . . Mrs. B. said to us . . . "Why do you want to adopt a child?" I said, "Well, you go to a church program, everybody's sitting up there watching their Mary or their Johnny. . . . You go to school, everybody is interested in my son or my daughter. . . ." All the way through life, isn't it? In high school, I mean, the parents, they have parents' nights because they're showing off their children . . . and if you haven't anybody, what have you got?*

MOTHER: *In fact, I think when you don't have children you do have an attitude of "Why can't those parents make that child behave? What is wrong with them?" I've always blamed the parent rather than the child, I've always felt it was the parent's fault if they wouldn't mind. But you find out when you have children of* your own—why you can't always get [hearty laughter] them to mind [everyone laughs]. As I said before . . . there are times when you wonder, have I spanked him too often? Or, if I spank him is it going to make him go out and do it again? Just to spite me, or this sort of thing. You have doubts. You're not too ready to blame parents. I used to say if I ever have kids, mine won't do that or be like that. Now I say, "I hope my kids won't do that."

There is satisfaction in the fact that they can provide a good physical environment and special experiences for the child.

MOTHER: Mmmhm, yes, when she brings any . . . of her friends . . . that's the first thing she does, is take them to her bedroom and show 'em her bedroom, you know . . . [short pause] the girls will say, "Oh, I wish I had a bedroom like this," they'd say to her, and then she feels pretty big . . . 'cause . . . she thinks she's got a good bedroom.

MOTHER: We've gone to Florida, and we went to California, and we went to Newport, and we went to Boston, and we went to Virginia, and we've had [child] all over the country, which hasn't hurt him any. . . . And we flew to Cuba, and I think that's good for him.

INTERVIEWER: These broadening experiences.

MOTHER: Yeah . . . that's helped him . . . I think that's done something for him.

INTERVIEWER: Helped him in what way?

MOTHER: Well, I think that it's probably helped him when he, ah, talks to some of the other children that he was afraid he wasn't on par with . . . that it just gives him a little more security and a little more, ah, he's not egotistical about it . . . but he just . . . he knows now that maybe he's not so bad off, you know . . . some of these other kids haven't had what he's got . . . you know . . . and in that way, I mean that I think that it helped him . . . because [child] needed something. . . .

INTERVIEWER: An extra something for his ego. . . .

MOTHER: That's right . . . and I think that this has helped him to do it.

But the attempts to teach the child are sometimes frustrating and disappointing because the child doesn't accept the teachings; the attempts to deal with everyday problems of child rearing end unsuccessfully, and the parent is left with a nagging, uncomfortable feeling of personal failure and guilt.

MOTHER: We're not doing him any good. 'Cause we don't know how to do him good. . . . If we could . . . whatever that is in his mind that makes him buck everything and refuses . . . he doesn't care anything about school. . . . He doesn't think he needs schooling. He's irresponsible, he doesn't care whether his clothes hang on him like a rag, or if his face is dirty or. . . . He cares about nothing. All he cares about is ice cream . . . dessert . . . and candy, oh, candy, candy and ice cream, television and comic books. Now these . . . the things he cares about . . . and that isn't enough to get by in this world.

MOTHER: Oh, I think the difficulty [laughs] is getting them to go in the direction that you want . . . I have in this particular case, uh, been a little disappointed in the poor showing in school . . . perhaps I accent that too much . . . because books are so very important to me . . . not that I'm a brain or anything . . . but I have a tremendous amount of faith in education. I have never been in awe of anyone with money . . . or social position . . . but I've always had a tremendous respect for intelligence . . . and learning is to me an exciting thing. . . . And when the children don't seem to be interested in this sort of thing at all . . . it's a frustration.

FATHER: I do feel very strongly on occasion . . . we would very much like to see the children succeed along these lines . . . one way as a reward to us . . . we can't see them . . . grow intellectually. . . .

MOTHER: Well, I think that I feel maybe we've failed her, you know . . . in not reaching her, ah, in giving her that security that she probably needed . . . because now she's getting older, it doesn't seem to be improving any . . . I often think, ah, I hope someday she does get someone that loves her a whole lot . . . you know . . . like maybe a husband that will . . . and that she can return that love to him, you know . . . I think about that. . . .

MOTHER: Oh, sometimes when I spank them and I shouldn't have . . . when I lose my temper with them . . . which happens every once in a while. And when I think I have been unkind to them. I feel ashamed.

One parent sums up with perceptive poignancy the feeling of dissatisfaction that comes with being a parent when things are going badly between parents and child.

FATHER: Well, I'll tell you many days . . . comes the day, in your position or mine, let's face it . . . I think the finest part of living is going home to your family . . . and I leave this office with that in mind . . . and I get to the end of our driveway and I sometimes end up saying, "Now why am I going home?"
INTERVIEWER: Hmmhmm.
FATHER: It's just that rough.
MOTHER: Isn't that a horrible feeling [in a low voice]?
INTERVIEWER: Yes, it is. It's a terrible feeling [long pause].

Satisfactions-Dissatisfactions: The Larger Family

For many of these children the family was larger than child and adoptive parents; it consisted of siblings and the extended family—grandparents, aunts and uncles, cousins, etc. Because they were adopted when older, the children were immediately able to act and interact, to solicit varying degrees of acceptance. Where it went well, the parents speak of the satisfactions they derive from the mutual acceptance between the child and siblings already in the home and between the child and members of the extended family.

MOTHER: There's a very close bond because the first year at the school picnic, I helped with that over at the park, and the girls were on the slides . . . [clears throat] excuse me . . . and this one boy came up and [sister] was at the top, and he was going to punch her . . . and [child] said, "That's my sister, you'd better not." [laughs]. And of course I saw it, and I got up because [child] would never have been able to handle this big boy . . . [laughs] but she tried . . . so I think there's a bond. . . .

FATHER: Oh yes, there's a bond there . . . they play together real good at times.

FATHER: We were up to the lake, you know, quite a bit this summer time. [Wife] and the kids were up there all during the Fourth of July, and those two kids played together, so help me Hannah, from morning till night, and while there might be one minor squabble during the day, but if there is one, it's all. Of course, they're both wonderful swimmers and divers and all that sort of thing, they both ski very well. . . . And, uh, they enjoy doing these things together.

MOTHER: [Child] does a lot of baby sitting with her niece and nephew, and this has been tremendous for her . . . because she loves those children and they just love her, and they're just like a little brother and sister to her . . . not like niece and nephew. Really . . . they're just like a sister and brother to her . . . and she doesn't get very much for baby sitting . . . she could pick up three times more from anybody in town . . . but she says, "But Mother, they are my relatives." I mean . . . this is her family . . . and once in a while I'll say, "Well, you don't have to do all that work when you go up to [aunt's] because it isn't expected of you. . . ." She does dishes and cleans up and does a lot of things. . . . "Well," she says, "Mother, it's my relatives." [laughs].

FATHER: Oh, [child] and Grandpa, they have become buddy, buddy.

MOTHER: They go out, and they hunt worms at night for fishing. . . .

FATHER: Oh, night crawlers, and go fishing together . . . oh. . . .

MOTHER: Because you know, Gramps isn't as spry as [child] and he can't get down there to do it, and [child] has an eye like a. . . .

He sees those worms and doesn't miss a one. Sometimes at night
. . . they catch this many in a coffee can. . . .

FATHER: All Grampa . . . has to do is holler out this hallway here
. . . "Hey, wanta go out and get night crawlers?" Boy, he's right
there. . . .

MOTHER: He's ah. . . .

FATHER: "Be right down." [Laughs, pause] Well, ah, my father had
a workshop in the basement . . . a workbench and tools, ah,
certain toys and things needing, ah, attention . . . those things
would come up in my absence . . . being at work, and of course
he being home here, "Grampa, would you fix this for me?" And
of course he would fix a little something or other, whatever the
case would be, and of course there became a kind of attachment
through that. . . .

MOTHER: . . . then [child] became interested in fishing and things
like that . . . and of course, Grampa had a cottage for a long time
. . . and he was a fisherman . . . and, ah, they would begin to
talk . . . fishing and sports . . . and of course [child] would take
Grampa his sports magazines and Gramps would give [child] his
. . . and the difference in years didn't seem to make much
difference.

The older child can reject, as well as accept, siblings and
extended family, and he can make this rejection clear.

MOTHER: . . . but [child] has been a little bit more cold, he is cold
to the rest of the family and even to making friends; he will go
into my mother's and walk through the kitchen without saying
hello or anything, he'll just walk into the front room and grab a
magazine or a catalog; he will sit on the davenport or the big
chair and there he'll sit until we're ready to go and not say a
word. It maybe isn't that he doesn't think as much of them as
[sister] does, but it's just maybe his nature. He doesn't say too
much to anyone in my family.

MOTHER: He always . . . plays [laughs] such darn mean little tricks
on [his sister] . . . I felt sorry she was . . . little . . . and then

he'd say, "[Sister]," he'd get in a tree, "[Sister] come here." And she'd of course come like a little dog, every time he called, she's right there . . . and she'd look up like that, and he'd spit in her face . . . [pause] . . . well, I thought there's one way of fixing that . . . I didn't say anything . . . right at that time . . . but then one time she was gonna help him . . . he was doing a little duty . . . up in the barn . . . I guess shoveling sawdust . . . and she was just . . . wanted to help 'im . . . so pretty soon she came . . . crying "Mom," she says, "he spit in my face." I said, "Why don't you spit right back." She says, "I can't reach him, he's too big." [Everyone laughs]. I went up there . . . he knew . . . he was coming around the corner . . . to see whether she had come in to tell me . . . and I grabbed him by the . . . by the arm . . . I says, "Here, you got him right here." I says, "Spit right at him." And then, ah, she did . . . she had a good aim, too . . . [laughs] and, oh, you could just see how that bothered him, and I says, "She felt the same way when you did it." I says, "It bothered her the same . . . [deep breath] as what it does you." And I didn't hear anything . . . about that . . . any more either. . . .

Satisfactions-Dissatisfactions: The Marital Relationship

The positive effects on the marital relationship which flow from the adoption also hold satisfactions for the parents.

MOTHER: It was better for our marriage because before that I worked, and we had quite a routine life and weren't so dependent on each other. I think probably if anything it probably brought us closer together because he had to spend a lot more time at home. [Husband] knew if I was going to keep my sanity, you know, it had to be a partnership deal all the way . . . I think that was one of the biggest things that really shook me is the fact that thinking that maybe something would happen to him and I didn't know if I could carry on without him.

FATHER: I think perhaps it did affect our marriage. We were not too aware of this probably, although I know we were getting rather self-centered as a couple, I don't mean individually. But as a couple we were rather self-centered and, ah, having the responsibility of a family, especially children that are older, as old as our boys were, it shortens up the time when you have to think about college and things like that, and so instead of thinking only in terms of our own needs, and our own desires, and our own future plans, we had to think of them, and I do think that we have come to understand each other a little better by watching the children and by deciding. We had to talk these matters of discipline and things like that . . . talk them over, so that we could agree and present a united front to the children. So we've done a little more talking probably and considering each other's point of view than we had before. Two adults can probably live with minor disagreements, but when there are children involved these disagreements have to be resolved before you can face the children. You have to be . . . if there's going to be any kind of discipline . . . you have to be united in effort. This is one change it has made in our understanding of each other and our points of view on some things.

Satisfactions-Dissatisfactions: The Community

The prestige accorded the adoptive parent by the community, and the acceptance by the community of the adoptive child are, of course, gratifying.

MOTHER: And they come to me and, uh, one lady not too long ago she said, I don't know, I wasn't expecting it, and she said "Well, I had to come and tell you, God bless you, what a wonderful thing you did to adopt those two girls." And it took me so, oh, by surprise. And still so many people have told me that that I should have got used to it but . . . it's always nice to hear.

MOTHER: Oh, it works out fine in the neighborhood. Ah, it was about a year later when one of his little friends said, "Gee, it seems like you were here all your life." See, we pick up these little things, and they really make us glad [laughs]. And, oh, he's in here. *Lots of friends. And the neighbors . . . everybody likes him, I just have to brag about him . . . all over. . . .*

This last satisfaction is unique to adoptive parents unlike most of those we have discussed, which are not. However, there are other satisfactions specific to adoptive parenthood, such as coping with the child's questions around adoption and the achievement by both parent and child of an accepting attitude toward adoptive status. The parents derive satisfaction in successfully preparing the child to handle questions and comments about adoption from schoolmates and playmates.

MOTHER: *Well, you know, children and many adults are, I don't think they want to be unkind, but many times say unkind things . . . well, you're just adoptive parents, and you're just adopted by these people. Before they went to school . . . before they went back to school after the holidays, I told them they would have this problem come up . . . that other children might say, "Well, you're just living there, and they are not your real parents." And I wanted them to have something to say. So I told them, after all, we picked you. We wanted you. These other children were born to their parents. They had to accept them, regardless. That satisfied them. They'd come home and say, "Mommy, so and so just said, well, you're just adopted, and we just told him, after all, our Mommy and Daddy wanted us. They wanted us to live with them and be theirs." So they had an answer.*

MOTHER: *And they would say, "How much did your parents pay for you?" And that we had an awful time with her. Until she ignored it, and then they quit. But it bothered her. She'd ask, "Did you buy me?" And I said, "Of course not." And I would explain. And, "Did you have to take me?" I said, "You tell some of these kids that their parents had to keep them. 'Cause they had them and they're their own. We didn't. We had you a whole year," and I said, "If we wanted to give you up any time during that year we could have done it." I said we wouldn't have had to keep you at all if we didn't want you. And I said you tell the other kids that their parents had to keep them. We didn't have to keep you. We kept you because we loved you. Well, she wasn't bothered much after that.*

General Satisfactions: Items of Family Folklore

Parents felt general satisfaction in seeing the growing solidarity of a family group composed of parents and children who had met each other relatively late in life. Some of the stories had apparently been recounted many times previously and had become part of a common family folklore which family members shared. The stories help further to indicate the nature of the feeling between these parents and children.

MOTHER: *He is slow in the way he does things . . . on Sunday morning I call the children for church, and they'd get up and I'd have their clothes ready for them, and then they were to get dressed and go to church . . . this one Sunday morning . . . [laughs] I went to the bottom of the stairs, and I called them, and it was, ah, just ten seconds after I called them and here [child] comes out the door with all his church clothes on . . . and I looked at him and finally I realized . . . he put his church clothes on the night before, including a dark green corduroy sport coat with a dress shirt and tie, and he slept in those clothes all night long . . . [laughs]. I said "[Child], what did you do? Did you sleep in your clothes?" And he looked at me, he was only half awake really . . . he looked at me and said, "How could you tell?" . . . [laughs]. He was wrinkled from top to bottom . . . he wanted to be ready on time. . . . See, [sister] was so quick she'd always be ready for church, "bingo," whereas [child] . . . it took a little longer to tie those shoes, a little bit longer to get that tie on . . . and here he was all dressed—he had slept in everything —even his shoes.*

MOTHER: *One day out in the kitchen she said, uh, to me, "Mother, who do you love the most, Daddy or [brother] or me?" And I said, "Oh, [child], I couldn't even begin to give you an answer to*

that because I love you all in a different way, each one of you."
She says, "Do you know who I love the best?" Well, I thought, I
don't know if I want your answer or not [laughs]. I said, "Well,
who do you?" Oh, she hesitated the longest time. I knew what
she meant. She didn't know if she should say [husband] or I, you
know. Finally she said, kinda low, she said, "First I love Daddy.
Then you. Then the hired man and then [brother]." [All laugh
uproariously.]

FATHER: You can see who's low man there.

FATHER: When it came time to buy a new car last year . . . the
boys had saved up . . . well, between them they had around
forty dollars, and so we went out to buy this car, and the first car
we looked at was a Chevrolet wagon or something. We looked at
the price in the window and boy, they both stood there looking
at the price and [child] said, "Nope, it's too much money."

MOTHER: He said, "It's too much money, we can't afford it."
[laughs].

FATHER: So finally, after awhile . . . we picked out this one and,
ah, how much would their forty dollars buy, that they'd buy this
or that of it, they finally decided they'd get all the door knobs.

———◄◆►———

Chapter 7

SPECIAL ADVANTAGES

AND DISADVANTAGES

OF ADOPTING

OLDER CHILDREN

The statements adoptive parents presented in the previous chapter mirror, for the most part, the experience of all parents. They express the satisfactions and dissatisfactions likely to be encountered in varying degrees by all parents. Some aspects of the parental experience, however, are different for this group of parents because they are adoptive parents and because the adoptive child was older when he came to them.

Advantages in Adopting Older Children

Some 66 per cent of the families noted the parent-child age difference is more appropriate in such an adoption; 33 per cent felt there was a distinct advantage in adopting a child old enough to participate in family activities upon his arrival; 20 per cent spoke of the fact that they avoided the drudgery of training a totally dependent infant; 14 per cent pointed to the advantages of being able to communicate and reason with a child old enough to have command of language; 13 per cent appreciated the fact that the child, having consciously experienced adoption, did not have to be "told" of this.

Many, coming as they did to adoptive parenthood relatively late in life, felt that the older child was the more appropriate choice for them. A preference for infants, expressed during the study period, is subject to modification as a result of the adoptive experience itself. Some who came expressing desire for an infant were able to accept the idea of adopting an older child at the end of the study period. Some who adopted the older child with some ambivalence became, as a result of the adoptive experience, strongly positive in their attitude about the desirability of older children for older parents because of age spread.

FATHER: *If you can have them from babies on, it's more like nature would have it, you know. But in our case, I'm really glad now that he was 5½ years old because we're getting older and, ah, it was better for our age. We didn't realize it as much at the time as we do now. I was talking to a party yesterday. He was, he's a little over 40, I guess, he's married and they've had 4 children in the past 5 years. We were kind of kidding him and he said, "Yeah, boy, I tell you, it's pretty hard to get down on the floor and play with these little brats already," he says. I says, "Yeah." When we adopted ours we were 35 before we put in our application, and our church home wouldn't even consider you at 35, but, you see, the state did. And I kinda think they know what they were doing because, ah, after all, we can tell now as we get older, you don't have the patience and that you do, you know, when you're younger.*

INTERVIEWER: *So if the parents are older it is an advantage to take an older child?*

FATHER: *I think it is.*

MOTHER: *Simply because one thing, when people get older, as [husband] and I have, I just don't think it's fair to the children to* take a baby. I mean, let's face it, why should that kid go around and say this gray-haired mother is my mother, when it could be the grandmother, why for instance now, in the wintertime if he wants to slide, come on mother, let's go sliding, and at my age I can still go down on the saucer or that little toboggan with him, and yet if we had gotten a baby four years ago, and I had waited 'til I was fifty to start going down the hill with him, well, who's going to start sliding down the hill at fifty years of age?

Not only is the older child more appropriate to the parents in terms of their own age but they are of a more appropriate age for fitting in with children of the parents' peer group of older adults. Their ages are more appropriate to the stage of the family life cycle of parents and friends of parents.

MOTHER: . . . and she fit into these social occasions that we had with our friends . . . they're still our best friends. The couple that we see perhaps most often has a girl just [child's] age and they're best friends . . . and, uh, I guess all our friends have children just about that age that she enjoys very much . . . and looks forward to being with and having come here. . . .

MOTHER: As for satisfactions, I think just having a child in common with your friends and their children makes for a very pleasant relationship, and we've just enjoyed doing things with kids always, so this has made it more fun for us to have one of our own to do it with. And the relatives, they have children about [child's] age which makes us glad, too, that he was older, because he fits in very well with, ah, the age range.

Parents spoke of the fact that the child is old enough to communicate his thoughts and feelings. He is capable of participating in many of the family activities and is, consequently, more stimulating and interesting to the parents, more responsive, more appreciative. As one parent said, in adopting an older child you have an "instant family." Infants are all potential; the older child has realized some of his potential.

While the older child requires more discipline, since he is more active and more capable of mischief, he is also easier to discipline; as one parent said, "You can explain to them why they can't do certain things, and you can reason with them . . . they are talkable children."

FATHER: You can build rapport more easily, I think. You have a youngster who can talk, and you got a youngster who can do things. . . . I mean . . . you get a tiny infant in the home, and they lay in the basket, or you take them out and jiggle them on your knee, or give them a bath and dress them and feed them, and that's just about the extent of it. Where you take the six- to eleven-year-old, these youngsters have already interests, and you can cultivate those interests, you can even build new interests. And this, I think to me, was the . . . was one of the nicest factors in working with this age group.

MOTHER: Babies are so routine, and you don't get much enjoyment out of them . . . you know, just sterilizing bottles and washing diapers, whereas I think someone older is much more interesting. Older people, if they would take an older child, would find it more enjoyable.

MOTHER: We were so delighted and, uh, I think actually I preferred the older age . . . because I have never found babies too interesting. And I know various friends . . . think this is very odd, maybe I don't have the right mother urge . . . or something, but I've always found babies rather dull . . . and I preferred an older child . . . I think that they're . . . they're at the age where you can really talk with them and work with them . . . and, uh . . . [child] is at an age now where I thoroughly enjoy her because she's beginning to reach out . . . to want to know answers to things. . . .

An older couple in our study group who first adopted an older child and subsequently adopted a younger child see the value of age-appropriate adoptions.

MOTHER: *Well, ever since we got* [younger child] *people think that* [father] *is his grandpa . . . you know, because, ah, because being so much older and that. . . . Even when you go to school, mothers and fathers of children that age are all young people . . .* [laughs] *you might say, some of them in their twenties . . . he probably thinks we're real old . . . though he never said anything.*

One of the corollary advantages that come with adopting an older child is that the parents receive the participation and assistance of the adoptive child in insuring the success of the adoption. Adjustment to infant adoption is a unilateral process which makes demands for accommodation on the parent alone. Not only is the older child capable of such an effort, he feels a desire to help make this venture successful. He himself may be desirous of, and capable of, initiating change in his behavior to vitiate the potentialities of conflict. The older child "adopts" the family as well as being adopted by the family. One parent said, "He was so happy to have a home I think he tried very hard to cooperate with us." Another said, "He was looking for parents so sincerely, you know, he wanted a mother and father so bad that he settled in much quicker than we expected."

FATHER: *Well, as I said before, ah, you have a child that wants to be adopted . . . like he did, and that's one thing in your favor. . . .*

INTERVIEWER: *The child wants it.*

FATHER: *And he knows it . . . I mean he's aware of it . . . that his folks can't keep him. He's already trying to adjust, because he wants to, and he's old enough to understand . . . to realize.*

MOTHER: *He tried so hard to enjoy the things that Daddy liked . . . baseball, bowling . . . and by that he grew to love . . . you know . . . and be liked.*

MOTHER: *Well, I, ah, we were worried about . . . at first, how we would adjust to the child, you know. . . . We didn't know quite how to speak to him or, you know . . . thought he'd feel strange, and it was just the opposite . . . the minute he entered our home we just forgot all about that . . . oh, I don't know . . . it's just a natural family . . . he adjusted so beautifully. . . . And the child made us overcome our feelings faster . . . [laughs] we adjusted too. . . . We were prepared to help him but he was helping us. He just . . . he made it easier for us.*

Of course, the problem lies in the conflict between the conscious desire to cooperate to insure acceptance in the home and the unconscious need to insure a repetition of rejection, express hostility to these parents in response to transference, test the parameter of parental acceptance, and resist acting lovingly with these parents out of fear of disloyalty to his own. But to the extent that the ego is capable of determining the child's behavior in terms which are relatively and rationally beneficial for the child, he will attempt to cooperate. A special advantage in adopting the older child is that he is old enough to make conscious decisions and to control his behavior accordingly.

Adopting the older child means acquiring a child who can feed and dress himself, is toilet trained, and has mastered many skills which make him independent of constant parental care. The drudgery of training a totally dependent infant does not exist. As one father noted, "To have a first child at our age is . . . rather rare, and so we didn't have to go through this diaper wash, 2 o'clock feeding, walk the floor bit . . . you see, our problems were different."

While the literature cites as a prime advantage for the adoptive parent the fact that the older child knows he is adopted, this is given surprisingly few times by the parents themselves— only 13 per cent of the parents mentioned this as a special advantage. "I think that's one advantage . . . of adopting an older child . . . the child knows it's being adopted . . . with an infant you . . . you'd always have to wonder, well, gee, when should I tell her, or should I ever tell her . . . and with the older child . . . it's just a fact when she comes. . . ."

Some of the special advantages in adopting an older child derive from the special difficulties, problems, and challenges which such adoptions present to the parents. If the older child is more likely to arrive emotionally damaged as a result of previous pathogenic living experiences, then "correcting" these emotional disabilities warrants self-congratulation and satisfaction.

If, as we shall cite below, one of the disadvantages in adopting older children is that they come with a configuration of living habits which need changing, then one of the advantages in adopting older children lies in the opportunity to help the children make such changes. If some need to be civilized before they can be socialized, then there is satisfaction in doing so successfully.

If the child has emotional ties to other parents and has a basis of comparing your parenting capacity with that of other parents he has experienced, then it is cause for great satisfaction if you can "win" the love and respect of such a child.

The advantages in adopting an older child that derived from the special challenge it presented was cited explicitly by some 11 per cent of the parents.

FATHER: *Well, I think that the child that age has some ability to do a certain amount of measuring you, and they're accepting you, while if you adopt a young child they accept you from the very beginning. And if you . . . if you adopt an older child, you have to measure up a certain amount to his . . . idea of what is a good parent. And, uh, I think if you can measure up, there's satisfaction in that.*

INTERVIEWER: *Um hmm. If you can measure up to the children and they accept you.*

FATHER: *Yes. And, uh, the children respect you and, uh, have affection for you, uh, it's a pretty good indication that you . . . you're doing the job that they . . . have a right to anticipate from you. While if a youngster starts, oh, natural children, or if you get a little bit of a youngster I don't think you have quite that, uh, that feeling. Those children have had that little experience . . . measuring you against . . . parents . . . or foster parents . . . while your own child, or a young child, won't be able to do that. You have the satisfaction that you have, uh, been able to, uh, win them over. By what you are and not just by the fact that they have always been with you.*

Additional advantages cited were that one is in a better position to know the kind of child you adopt when you accept an older child, and that the older child's school attendance permits an easier adjustment to adoptive parenthood. One parent said, "It takes a little pressure off you . . . till you get used to him. In the beginning you're under constant 24-hour pressure, but if they go to school it relieves you for a while, and that's the way you break into it."

Some 10 per cent of the parents expressed the view that in taking an older child they are performing a special service. One put it this way, "You might have a little halo around your head for taking somebody that, eh, isn't quite so apt to be taken by everybody." Another said, "I mean you feel that you've done, ah, a little something extra . . . that so many don't want the older ones." A third said, "Well, we have the satisfaction, I would say, of feeling that we have given a child a home who didn't have much of a chance to have one otherwise."

One person noted that in adopting an older child you were absolved from responsibility for some of the difficulties which the child presented—absolved to an even greater extent than adoptive parents might generally feel they are because of blameworthy factors attributable to others.

MOTHER: . . . *she did wet at school a couple times. And, of course, then we wondered what some of the people thought, you know, afterwards we decided she . . . well, she was what she was, and she was older when we got her and everything, it wasn't our fault to a certain extent that it was going on . . . she was kind of a big girl already when she came and . . . living the way she lived before, she couldn't help a lot of her ways.*

Some additional advantages became clear as we discussed with the parents the adjustments required in their lives by the accession of children. Sociologists concerned with the family have identified some of the strain imposed on marriage by virtue of the birth of a baby and becoming a parent (17, pp. 196–201, 33, pp. 367–72, 46, pp. 352–55).

The penalties are economic, social, psychological, and physical. A considerable adjustment is required in the budget, leisure time activity, living patterns, and the allocation of affection between husband and wife.

Many of the adjustments result from the fact that the infant child, biological or adoptive, is a completely helpless and dependent human being. Since the older child is not helpless and dependent, many of the adjustments required of the first-time parent were not demanded of these adoptive parents. Their social life after adoption was not sharply different. They continued to do many of the same things and merely included the child.

MOTHER: *Our activities weren't changed much by having him. We go to a movie now and then . . . we take him to a movie and quite a few of the Walt Disney pictures . . . he loves those so much. Well, we enjoy them too. I would say the only thing would be we wouldn't stay as late . . . we would come home earlier . . . if he was along, and things like that . . . you know.*

FATHER: *I don't say we never left 'em . . . we'll go out without them at times. . . . But the majority of the time they go with us . . . whenever we go somewhere.*

MOTHER: *As a matter of fact I think they probably enhanced our . . . our going, because, ah, because we'd go to picnics . . . and swimming. . . . Do some more family things . . . we would plan pick-up suppers and go out to the beach . . . or we'd take them to the carnival or circus . . . which we ourselves would never have managed . . . it was wonderful . . . [laughs]. So probably we went a little bit more than we had before.*

Some explanation for the fact that adjustment to parenthood was not a major problem for these parents lay in the fact that parenthood came to them relatively late in their life cycle. Most parents first become parents in their early twenties. These adoptive parents became parents in their late thirties and early forties, when they were already established in their careers, and their earning capacity was at a relatively high level. The financial burdens occasioned by parenthood could be borne without great difficulty. Furthermore, adoption by older parents comes at a time when their life is likely to be contracting somewhat, when social life is likely to be more limited. These parents, then, found it less burdensome than younger parents in staying close to home in caring for the child.

Parenthood came in the tenth to fifteenth year of the marriage. Parents were secure and comfortably habituated to each other after years of marital interaction. They were not so likely to be threatened by some affection being withdrawn from them and directed toward the child or to feel dissatisfied if they had less time alone together.

The infant's schedule may be very different from that of the adult world around him. This is less true of the older child. He eats at the same time and place as the adults, and he eats the same food. His going to sleep and waking up patterns are already similar to those of adults. The nature of his activities is somewhat similar. An older child can be much more smoothly integrated into an adult-oriented daily schedule than can an infant.

Perhaps these factors help to explain the limited number of dissatisfactions expressed about an adjustment one might suppose would occasion many problems. Parents did have problems in adjusting to parenthood but they tended to regard them as minor, inevitable and acceptable concomitants of having children. This was a small price to pay for the satisfaction of parenthood.

Disadvantages in Adopting Older Children

The recurrent difficulties mentioned by parents during the interviews suggest some of the particular disadvantages in adopting an older child: 60 per cent of the parents mentioned that the child had been molded by others during an earlier period in his life, and they were faced with the problem of changing patterns of behavior to which the child had become habituated; 50 per cent pointed to the fact that such children, having lived under stressful circumstances, come to adoption with some emotional difficulty; 45 per cent noted that they found it hard to understand the child, since one has only limited knowledge of his previous life and experience; 29 per cent of the families expressed some disappointment at having missed the joys and pleasures of growing with the child from his early infancy; and 24 per cent felt anxious about some competition with the other parental figures the child had known and loved.

Many of these special problems and disadvantages of older adoptions are reflected in the sentence completion material. Thus, in response to the stub "When you adopt an older child [parents answered]

   . . . there may be more problems in getting close to the child."

   . . . there are some difficult times ahead for the parent because most of them are probably insecure."

   . . . you must grow up to where the child is all at once instead of growing up with them."

   . . . some time must be spent to develop the love that grows with association."

   . . . it worries you a little more as to how they will adjust to you."

   . . . you have to correct other peoples' mistakes as well as your own."

   . . . you must be extra patient and tolerant. They need more love and reassurance."

In response to the stub "Adoptive children [parents wrote]

   . . . require more love and affection because they want to be sure they belong."

   . . . must be shown extra love."

   . . . often have had problems and need to be understood."

And in response to "Being an adoptive child [they noted]

. . . must be difficult; the adjustment and fear must be astronomical."

. . . is very difficult for an older child with a good memory. It is hard to leave everything and start anew."

. . . their past is definitely a real problem for them to overcome."

. . . from my experience are very insecure and always seem to be on the defensive."

One aim of the study was to provide social workers and prospective adoptive parents with fuller knowledge of special problems faced by the parents of the older adoptive child and their methods of coping with them. In line with this we present a more extended discussion of the major recurrent problems through illustrative excerpts regarding these problems. We start with those that appear to have been encountered less frequently.

Since the child is older the disadvantage is that you have him as your child for only a limited period.

MOTHER: *I'd put him back six years again, ten years, so that I could start all over and bring him up again. He's gonna get away from me too soon.*

FATHER: *They grow up so quick. And when you get 'em like [child], he was ten when we got him and now he's sixteen, and he's going to high school a couple years . . . pretty soon he'll be out of high school and grown up, and it seems that you don't get time to really know 'em . . . I mean the time is very short there. Time goes so fast, I mean, they grow up.*

The older child is more aware of his environment, more capable of receiving and interpreting the messages from his immediate environment; this imposes a strain on the parent. Parental mistakes which the infant would miss do not get by the older child. As one mother said, "And when they come as children of that age . . . you don't have a chance to feel each other out . . . I mean, they're just, ah, constantly aware of what you're doing. . . ."

The nature of the affective relationship which one can develop with the older children is different, some parents note.

MOTHER: *Well, like I say, I don't think that I've actually had the closeness and the affection, I mean, I don't think they, oh, I don't know what word to use, that you would have for your parent if you were brought up from a baby onward, where you have all that tender, loving care when you're a baby that you can't give them when they're older, so actually I don't think it's natural for them to have that feeling, do you? I don't think so.*

INTERVIEWER: *It's very difficult to develop that feeling.*

MOTHER: *Yeah. Because I got to get to know you, I mean, you're absolute strangers when you see one another, to go into somebody's home that you never met before it's. . . . Like I say, by the time you get acquainted he's ready to be independent, and at that age it's not his fault completely.*

A very intense relationship develops out of the total dependency of the infant on the mothering figure. This kind of relationship is inappropriate between the older child and adoptive parents.

Similarly, another mother was disappointed that the child was so self-sufficient that the woman could not physically get close to her. She coped with the problem by encouraging some regression on the part of the child to develop a physical dependency which permitted a more intense affectional relationship.

While older children can be more communicative and participate in family activity, younger children are less blasé and more spontaneously enthusiastic about whatever experiences the parents offer. One parent said, "You know how up-in-the-air a young kid can get. They show pleasure more than the older child."

While some cited the fact that the child was shared with the school so soon after coming as an advantage, others felt this to be a disadvantage. "You had so little time with him once he started school that it was hard to get to know him intimately." The older child is more easily recognized by people who have seen him before, and this is a disadvantage. The fact that, unlike an infant, he has lived in the wider community means that there is a greater pool of people who are likely to recognize him.

MOTHER: About the first year we had him, see, we had a centennial across the street in this field . . . thousands of people from all over . . . and a cousin of his saw him and recognized him. He said, "Aren't you H _____ K _____?" So he says, "No, I used to be, but my name is M _____ R _____ now. I live across the street." So the cousin, then, they told the grandmother. And she writes to him and tells him where his brothers are and all this sort of thing.

And while some parents cited as an advantage the fact that one received the child after the period of total dependency was past, others saw this as a disadvantage. Twenty-nine per cent of the parents said in one way or another that they missed the joy and pleasure which comes from growing with a child from the start.

FATHER: You know, there's a lot of difference between an infant and an older child, though many of the problems are already passed over. I mean, certainly some of the joys are missing too . . . this business of the first shot, and the first teeth, and getting up at night and so on, you miss all of that, because maybe you're not really parents unless you have those experiences.

MOTHER: Well, as far as we're concerned I feel it was a disadvantage not to have had her sooner, but there would be the advantage . . . if some people would want to call it that . . . I don't feel that way . . . but skipping those first five years you wouldn't have had the responsibility, but what real mother and father wouldn't prefer having that? One of the cutest things [child] said *after she was here several months . . . one day I was singing to her and she was lying on a pillow and she said, "Oh, Mommy," she said, "You know one thing I feel so bad about?" And I said, "What do you feel so bad about?" And she said, "I only wish you could have had me right from the beginning." So. . . . And I wish I could have had her right from the beginning too.*

IGNORANCE OF CHILD'S PAST

The parent meets the older adoptive child late in the latter's childhood. He has done much and experienced much before the genesis of his life as a child to these parents. They talk of the void which exists for them regarding the earlier life of the child, which they have not and can never really fully share. There are gaps in their knowledge and understanding of what went into forming this child. Sometimes the child's behavior is a puzzle they cannot hope to solve because the keys to the solution are not available. Also, there is a sense of discontinuity, as though one came in on the middle of a story; and while some of the general background is provided by the agency, the details remain vague or unknown.

It has implications for the parents' behavior in regard to the child. They are uncertain of how their standards will effect what response in the child. The response is partly triggered by experiences about which they may know little. Forty-five per cent of the parents noted this discontinuity as a problem.

MOTHER: *He had a tendency, not really bad . . . but he had a tendency towards telling an exaggerated story . . . well they were lies, nothing harmful, but they were lies. And you couldn't always get to the bottom of the truth. Now somewhere along the line he felt it necessary to lie. Where? What? When? I don't know his past experiences that well. How can I understand why he does this? Because why is he lying? Why does he feel that it's necessary? I've never done anything to frighten him, why does he feel he must lie to me about things that don't matter? And if you knew, say for instance, that his grandfather beat him, I don't know, maybe his grandfather punished him quite severely for something he did so that he thought, "Well, I won't let that happen again, I'll tell a lie to them."*

MOTHER: *And you'd kind of like to know when they started to walk, or talk. This is one thing that came up that I can think of . . . he asked me, ah, "Why does [baby sister] suck her thumb or want to suck her fingers all the time?" When I said, "Well, I'm sure you must have sucked them when you were a little boy," and he said, "How would you know?" You know, he knows he wasn't ours when they were little. "Oh, I never did." And he thinks he's got one up on you [laughs]. . . . "Oh, I didn't." Well, I'm sure you did." But, ah, they feel as though they have . . . secrets . . . of course, I think all children should have secrets, but, ah, you'd like to know. Well, did they suck their fingers?*

A particular manifestation of this general problem of discontinuity was the puzzlement sometimes encountered regarding the child's health background—20 per cent of the parents mentioned this.

MOTHER: *We still have to ask her when somebody says, "Did your daughter have measles or something, so that you'd better not let her in," so I have to say, "L _____, do you remember having them?" Because I don't know.*

MOTHER: *[Child] has to wear glasses . . . now maybe if we had known that he had the red measles, maybe we would have watched his eyes a little bit better, because we took him to a specialist and he said, he just said, "Uh huh, this is the result of the red measles," so there we were . . . and you know how little children are . . . they won't tell you . . . if they can't see.*

ADJUSTMENTS TO PARENTHOOD

We mentioned, in discussing advantages of older adoption, that adjustment to parenthood was less likely to be problematic because of the age of the child, the age of the parents, and the time in the life cycle of the marriage and of the career when such adoptions occurred.

Yet some of these same factors are occasions for difficulty in adjusting to parenthood. Having a child late in the life cycle and late in the cycle of the marriage meant changes in habits that had become somewhat rigid because they had been maintained without change for a long period.

MOTHER: *Yes, yes . . . that makes a big difference, ah, I was very particular about everything . . . and, I mean, my drawers just had to be right, and my husband's drawers just had to be right, and everything had to be just right, and of course after I had the children, that's changed to a certain degree. . . . I didn't have time for all that foolishness. . . . There are times I get a little rattled if it's gone too far . . . [laughing]. I've got to admit that . . . although the kids now . . . they both . . . they, ah, help me tremendously.*

MOTHER: *Oh, there was probably an adjustment to make, uh, you want to talk on the telephone and that's just the time when the children argue about who's going to write something . . . you know, or arguing over some toys . . . these were the things that we'd never contended with before. . . . And with W_____ riding on his bike and P_____ running back and forth and playing ball and stuff on our lawn . . . it suddenly began to look like the neighbor's yard did . . . and these were pretty difficult adjustments to make; we didn't say anything . . . I mean that's . . . we figured . . . that's part of being a child. Of course we still tried to restrict them where they wouldn't destroy, uh, you know, at the flower garden and . . . but it was difficult to see some of the things we held so dear . . . suddenly common property.*

And with children come noise and loss of privacy—a loss which older parents are perhaps less well equipped to accept.

MOTHER: *Quiet! That's what I miss the most. A lot of days I found . . . we have a piece of land that goes out in the marsh . . . and I can go way out there on the end by myself and just . . . sit and get away from all this confusion and noise . . . but this is something that natural parents go through too. . . . It was a shock. The social worker had said to me in the interviews, "We want you to think this over very well . . . have you thought of the noise that there will be." And I made the remark that, Oh, the laughter of children was like tinkling bells . . . and as I say to some of my friends now . . . it almost drives me crazy . . . at times . . . you know, this laughter is no longer tinkling bells.*

Like all first-time parents these parents had to cope with anxiety engendered by their ignorance about the details of child life.

MOTHER: *I thought I knew quite a bit about them before, about children, until I got some of my own, and I found out I knew absolutely nothing. I knew how to feed them, change their clothes, clean them up, and take care of a little baby, but you don't know anything about their development. Like what about two boys who like to go around dirty all the time. You know . . . well, I didn't know for sure. I went and talked to some of my friends who had children. Well, they said this is their development up to a certain age.*

FATHER: *Until they get to be interested in girls [Laughs].*

MOTHER: *Well, that's no joke. And some of them don't even clean up then. Our children for instance, do children sit and brood occasionally? Do they play all the time or do they sit around once in a while and do nothing? These things I didn't know. I had to go and ask. 'Cause he didn't know either.*

FATHER: *Oh, I knew some things, but you know you didn't always ask the right questions [laughs].*

Becoming a parent late in marriage and when older carries the financial advantage cited above, that of accepting the burden of parenthood when the earning capacity of the husband was high. It also implied a disadvantage, however. Since many of the adoptive mothers had been without children in the home they had been free to work. These were two-income families which, with the accession of the child, became one-income families. In six cases parents mention some of the pressures felt because an income-producing mother left work to become a full-time parent.

MOTHER: *Well, of course, before we've been kind of free as a butterfly, as the old saying goes. And now . . . and we had been pretty self-centered, you know, and when we wanted to go we went, because both of us were working; we had two salaries and when you have two salaries you have extra money to spend. When they came in, we just had to stop that.*

FATHER: *I think it would be important to say here that—unless somebody gets the wrong idea—that this was a delight to make this change. And this was not something that we were sad about, that we didn't get to run around. . . .*

MOTHER: *We had lots of fun with them. . . .*

FATHER: *We sure did. . . .*

MOTHER: *I think one of the things that we have . . . given up . . . probably more by me, ah, as I'm wearing one of [husband's] old sports shirts . . . and, ah, the reason I'm wearing it is because it's long enough that it covers up the back of my slacks, which are worn thin to the point where it would be dangerous not to wear something this length. And I think this is, ah, this is a big item. . . .*

FATHER: *We went from two incomes . . . to one . . . and that's not easy.*

MOTHER: *I'd kid them about the slacks that I'm wearing. . . . And I pointed out to them . . . I said, "Well, if you little 'rumbums' weren't here, well, maybe I'd have a new pair of slacks—but then I wouldn't have you to, ah, [long pause] to fuss with."*

These were some of the specific adjustments adoptive parents mentioned that they had to make in accepting the role of parenthood. By and large, however, the general impression given is that the older child presents the parents with fewer problems and less of a need to break sharply with the past configuration of life patterns than is true when becoming a parent to an infant.

PREVIOUS SOCIALIZATION EXPERIENCES

A frequently cited disadvantage in adoptive parenthood of older children relates to the fact that the child, when he comes, has an established pattern of behaviors which are the result of socialization to another family's "culture." This was mentioned by 60 percent of the parents.

MOTHER: *Oh,* [sighs] *well . . . the adjustment is harder than with an infant . . . that you can expect because the child is, ah, already . . . take like . . .* [child] *. . . here . . . they have ways of their own . . . I don't know how to explain that either . . .* [laughs].

INTERVIEWER: *Um hmm* [pause].

MOTHER: *They're a little harder to, ah, manage, because . . .* [pause].

FATHER: *It's hard to teach an old dog new tricks. . . .*

MOTHER: *Yes . . . that's for sure. They've already . . . are sort of set in their ways . . . the way they've been going . . . where an infant just naturally grows according to, ah, infant of course just naturally grows the way you bring them up . . . just like your own, you know. . . . And these already have . . . had some training probably . . . some ways in which we don't even like . . . and you've got to break them of those habits. . . .*

MOTHER: *I think it's easier for a younger child because you sort of . . . you teach them your way. . . .*

INTERVIEWER: *Surely.*

MOTHER: *Where you get an older child, ah, like with* [child] *he had been in three different homes . . . and he was just so mixed up, ah, "I did it this way," you know, and "I did it this way, I did it*

that way, and now you want me to do it this way." "What am I
supposed to do?"

It is a problem for the child because he is confused by the
different patterns of doing the same thing which he has to learn
and unlearn. It is an emotional difficulty for the child because
the different behavioral responses are tied, affectively, to the
different parent-teachers with whom he has identified in learning such responses and whom he now has to deny in giving up
such responses. It is a problem for the parents because initially
they have to tolerate and accept what is, in terms of their own
standards, the unacceptable behavior which the stranger has
brought into their family circle.

The parents pointed out that at least for a time you "had to
grit your teeth" and live with the fact that the child "had to
have some time to learn your way of living," and you have to
"put up with these things until they come around to accept
your ways of doing it."

The parents further face the difficult problem of showing
acceptance of the child but rejecting his behavior in initiating
the process of changing it.

FATHER: *The problem is to, ah, [sigh] I suppose to be able to*
accept that child fast enough so that there isn't a lapse . . . in
there, where the child feels she might not be wanted . . . to be
able to give the child the feeling of being wanted, of love . . .
yet here's a stranger with totally different habits, maybe a totally
different vocabulary, a way of expressing things that isn't yours
. . . and . . . not to, ah, be too critical. Because they're old
enough at this age to resent criticism, to get this thing changed
without being too critical and yet to make them feel they're
wanted and loved.

Parents spoke of the specifics of the process of helping the
child "fit in" to the "culture" of the adopted family. The
"disjoint" between child and family identified most frequently

by the parents lay in the area of language and feeding habits, less frequently in the patterns of sleep schedules and leisure time activity, and only rarely were ideological-philosophical differences noted.

As one listened to the parents talk about fitting the children into the family, the transition seemed to be not so much from one home to another but rather from one class culture to another. Almost all of the children had come from a lower-class family and had been placed in a middle-class family. It was the difference in the behavior patterns of the two class groups which required changing as the children were displaced upward.

Children came with a "pretty earthy" vocabulary which needed to be censored for acceptability in a middle-class milieu. Their speech was grammatically offensive to middle-class ears, replete with double negatives and "aints." They were less apt to use expressions of politeness more characteristic of the well behaved middle-class child so that parents had to remind them constantly of their "pleases" and "thank yous."

The meals preferred by these children featured hot dogs, hamburgers, beans, and cokes. What could be cooked quickly, or what came out of a can, were apt to be familiar. Green vegetables and salads were likely to be rejected because they were unfamiliar. Once again these are differences between a lower-class diet and a middle-class diet.

It was not merely a question of the kind of food the children were ready to eat, it was also the way food was eaten. Table manners needed changing, and beyond this there was a subtle difference in the schedule, timing, and context in which meals were eaten.

MOTHER: *They had been raised in town, had been allowed to run free. If they didn't want to go home for a meal nobody went to look for them, and if they wanted to live on just a can of beans and maybe some wieners or something like that, that was O.K., too.*

FATHER: . . . and the kids, when we first had 'em, we'd call 'em and they "weren't hungry," and "I don't want to eat now, I'll eat later." There was no such thing as mealtime, in their home.

MOTHER: And now the social worker told us that . . . she didn't think [child] had ever eaten at a table before he came to our house. . . . When he was walkin' around, he just picked what he could find, from cupboard or shelf or refrigerator or whatever it was. . . . And he never sat at a table to eat.

In the adopting middle-class homes meals were apt to be scheduled. The family came together at a stated time for meals and sat down at a table, observing the familiar mealtime rituals of polite table manners. Sleep schedules had been equally haphazard and irregular, some of the children having been permitted to remain up to watch late T.V. shows, putting themselves to sleep whenever they felt ready. Differences in cleanliness habits also may reflect distinctions of class patterns.

MOTHER: And another thing, when we first got her she didn't wash and have a bath. Did she have to be washed at night before she went to bed? And she would get so dirty! She didn't know what a bath is . . . meant or why.

FATHER: Why brush her teeth? Or why should she bathe?

MOTHER: Why should she wash before she goes to bed, and I'd say, "Well look at your feet and your legs." "Never washed when I was home." I said, "You mean you'd crawl in the white sheets like this?" "Sheets? We never had sheets."

MOTHER: She couldn't understand why she couldn't go in the bathroom when [husband] was in there. And [husband] just couldn't explain. He said, "Decent people just don't do that young lady." He said, "You're just going to have to get used to it because you are never going into the bathroom with me."

MOTHER: Well, she took a shower for a long time without any soap . . . [laughs]. . . . All of a sudden I found out she wasn't using *any soap . . . [laughs] . . . she said she didn't know she was supposed to use soap when she took a shower . . . see? Little things like that. . . .*

These children were less careful about keeping their rooms in order, hanging up their clothes, changing underwear regularly, or using shoe polish—and they had to be trained in cleanliness and neatness.

The lower-class orientation toward present gratification in an environment with an uncertain tomorrow needed to be changed in a new environment more certain to provide tomorrow the pleasures that one does not snatch today. The transition was from an orientation concerned with present, immediate gratification to a postponement of gratification and an orientation toward the future.

MOTHER: *She had to learn that candy and cookies and those sorts of things are there to be eaten, but they have to use a little prudence with it and not just gobble it down as if there's not going to be another day. That's maybe because they didn't have it sitting around . . . they would all be gone that afternoon. Because maybe there wouldn't be any there tomorrow. I think they found that there is a tomorrow.*

Changing children's habits to fit into adoptive family patterns was made less difficult for many because the children had undergone some retraining by middle-class foster parents. Adoptive parents spoke with gratitude of the debt they owed to foster parents. The foster home is, in effect, the older child's preparatory school for adoptive family living.

MOTHER: *She had been for two years in a foster home where she had very good training. Well, she ate nicely and she used nice English . . . no swearing . . . she was polite and that sort of thing. She had been exposed to this so that we didn't have any problems at all as far as that was concerned, and I'm sure a great deal of it was due to the home in which she had been placed.*

Although a sizable number of parents mentioned that they had to help the child change some habits, almost none saw this as a particularly difficult or persistent problem. Most of the old ways yielded easily to the examples set by adoptive parents. They were apparently shed by the children without great trauma after a transitional period of adjustment.

PREVIOUS AFFECTIVE TIES

A recurrently cited disadvantage in adoption of older children was the child's psychological ties to other families, roots in other families, and the division of affection which this implies. Although this is generally regarded as one of the most serious problems in older adoptive child-parent relationships, it was mentioned by only 24 per cent of the group. One could claim that the very infrequency with which it was explicitly mentioned as a problem tends to confirm its importance to the parents. Keenly sensitive to the impact of competing affective ties the parents deliberately avoid the pain which might be occasioned by raising this problem for discussion. Those who spoke of it did so with intense concern.

Children also faced the problem of coping with affective ties to former parents and siblings. On a conscious level, the parents' desire that the child forget the past was supported and reinforced by the child's own need to resolve past attachments and invest himself emotionally in his new parents. Based on parents' reports of the child's questions about his life before adoption, the memories he shared with the parents, the problems raised by earlier commitments, and the efforts at coping with such problems we categorized the child's adjustment to such ties as "resolved," "latent," or "unresolved." In 18 cases the information was not sufficiently clear to permit categorization.

Children whose ties to the past we characterized as resolved showed some evidence that they had talked out such memories, according to their parents. They seemed comfortable in bringing up memories of the past and did not seem to be made unduly anxious by such memories or to erect any defenses against them. The problem had been resolved with free expression of feeling about the past. They have also permitted themselves some overt expression of hostility against their parents for having neglected them. Few significant residuals from these conflicts seemed to intrude on current functioning.

These assessments, it is important to note, are based on the parents' reports and hence not only on what parents are ready to speak of, but also on their sensitivity to the child's behavior. Subtle manifestations of conflict if unperceived or misinterpreted by the parents could not, and would not, have been reported.

MOTHER: *Of course, every night for about six weeks I would sit on their bed and talk to them because they had a lot of things they wanted to get off their minds, and that's what they did. But I don't think they were upset about it . . . they wanted to know more about it. . . .*

INTERVIEWER: *What kinds of things were they concerned about that you found necessary to discuss?*

MOTHER: *Well, they wanted to know about their real, their first mother, their family, their brothers and sisters, that sort of thing, and they wanted to know how long it would take before they could be legally our adopted children, you know, that type of thing. There was a lot of questions that they wanted to ask and hadn't felt free to ask before, and those were the questions that they had to get all straightened out.*

MOTHER: *She's real curious about her parents and why they left them. She can't figure out why their parents left them. And so I explain all about how some people can't take care of their children and that's what adoption is for. And she listens and she asks questions and talks about it. And she tells me some of the things she remembers and once she just got real resentful and she said, "And I know whose fault it is too!" And, oh, she was mad, and she doesn't get that mad too often, and I said, "Who?" And she said, "Well, these big people that have no business having 'em and then leaving 'em. Well, boy, I wouldn't leave my children," you know, oh, she thinks that's just awful. She thinks that that's just terrible that adult people would want to have children and then give 'em away and leave 'em.*

MOTHER: *I feel, uh, very sure that she expressed herself freely what she thought. She wanted to tell her family history.*

INTERVIEWER: *She did want to talk about it?*

MOTHER: *Oh, yes. Very much. I never had to ask. It just seemed that for the first year that she just . . . worked hard at trying to remember everything. In the first year she just talked and talked, even when she was visiting us. From the time that she met us. I believe that she felt that freedom with us. And she just seemed to get it out of her system.*

The children whose relationship to past ties we categorized as latent seem to have resolved the problem on the basis of conscious suppression or unconscious repression. These children, according to the parents, had never mentioned their past and never asked questions about it. It was, for them, to be studiously avoided. They never took the initiative in introducing this kind of material but if, as a result of some happenstance, the question did arise they reacted with discomfort and anxiety and actively sought to end the discussion. On the other hand, the defenses they had established seemed effective in permitting them to make the affectional transition to a positive relationship with the adoptive parents.

The adjustment was labeled latent since there seemed to be some possibility, in these cases, that at some time in the future the question of the past might come up again for a more definitive resolution. The adjustment seemed successful, in that it permitted them to fulfill adequately the social and emotional demands of the child's role to the adoptive parents, yet it did not seem as complete and final a solution as that attained by the group of children discussed above.

These children had not fully come to terms with their past; they had found a way of walling it off and had delayed a final consideration of their memories. It may well be that a final consideration may never prove to be necessary, that conscious and/or unconscious "forgetting," may be sufficient to permit these children to live out their childhood, and perhaps their lives, without such memories disturbing their relationship with others. From our limited vantage point, seeing only the small segment of their lives which we glimpsed through the eyes of the parents, the suppressive-repressive modes of coping were sufficient to enable the child to establish a satisfying relationship with the adoptive parents.

FATHER: *But she don't recall too much about them, uh, or should I say she doesn't, well, it doesn't creep into her conscious mind very much. When something comes up she knows it. Occasionally she has to stop and think. We ask her about it and she's rather . . . rather vague. Apparently she has made an effort to kinda forget about the past.*

MOTHER: *Ahhh [sighs] . . . well, there are times, yes, but . . . [sigh] . . . it happened with our daughter, the same with the boy. We told them all about being adopted and that. I believe it was a week or two after . . . no, it was when we went to court with the kids, that's when we told them. And, ah, then they both expressed a desire that they never wanted to hear nothing about it again. And it has been a closed topic in our home. We never . . . we never mention it, and if they would talk to us about it we would talk to them about it. But as long as they don't bring it up themselves, we do not bring it up to them. And we told the both kids, if it ever came . . . the . . . there ever was a day that they want to know more about it or there was any questions they had, they should surely to come to us, so we certainly would tell them.*

And they both said, as far as they were concerned we were their parents and that was it.

INTERVIEWER: This was years ago, then.

MOTHER: That was years ago. And since then, they have never asked one question, neither one.

FATHER: He talks of his blackened past, he was mighty glad to get rid of it. . . .

MOTHER: [Breaking in] He didn't . . . want any part of it. Chuck it . . . I don't want to remember any of that.

FATHER: Bury it . . . bury it.

MOTHER: What she remembers isn't too pleasant to recall, and consequently she has no desire to even talk about it, because she doesn't exactly have any happy memories at all. She said, "Oh, well," she said, "let's just forget about the whole thing." So that we drop it there. If at any time, oh, it hasn't been for a year and a half or so, but once in a while she'd reminisce a little bit and she'd say "Do you want to hear about it?" [laughs]. And I'd always say, "Well, if you want to talk about it." And she'll go on a little bit and she'll say, "Oh, let's forget the whole thing." So then we forget it.

INTERVIEWER: You just let her set the pace.

MOTHER: That's right. I haven't questioned her because I don't . . . she'll offer whatever she wants to tell . . . and it really isn't that important to me.

MOTHER: Because the thing that piqued our curiosity was that [child] has never mentioned his mother. I kept waiting for him to talk about his mother . . . he talked about his father . . . and he mentioned his grandmother, several times and, of course, his brothers and sisters. He mentioned often they were all older than he, but mother, the mother was never mentioned.

INTERVIEWER: And you couldn't help but wonder why.

MOTHER: And we couldn't help but wonder why, and there've been times when I've felt that he rejected me because I was a woman and his mother was a woman and that rejection . . . of her carried over to me. Now, as I say, this is why we have some curiosity about her and wonder just what happened to her.

A third categorization covered those children who still manifested active and unresolved emotional ties—either to natural or foster parents. In a few instances, while active and unresolved, such ties did not occasion undue difficulty in the parent-child relationship, although it created a problem for the parents.

In these instances there appeared to be a complicated transactional relationship between the nature of the child's emotional response to the memories and the parents' level of tolerance, acceptance, understanding, and ego strength. If a parent could accept a high level of provocative competition before reacting negatively to the child then even the active intrusion of past parents could not threaten the relationship.

In some instances active and unresolved memories did threaten the relationship between adoptive parents and the child. Often the interference with the establishment of new affectional relationships was so blatant that even the most accepting and understanding of parents were unable to cope adequately. The memories need not have been positive; as a matter of fact they may have been exceedingly negative, but by actively determining the child's behavior they prevented the establishment of a satisfying relationship in the adoptive home.

MOTHER: *But then you would think, when she has this question of, ah, why did my parents give me up, that she would accept somebody who accepts her . . . wouldn't you? But she doesn't. We tried to explain to her about the birth certificate. "The law is all wrong . . . you can't . . . they can't put your name down there as my mother and father . . . they've no right to do that on my birth certificate." I mean at every turn you come back to this same problem.*

INTERVIEWER: *Mmmhmm. So that in her mind she doesn't accept you as her mother and father.*

MOTHER: *No. Never has, from the . . . as soon as she came.*

FATHER: *One thing . . . we do know, ah, that she remembers her parents. We have had some very, very serious discussion that* went into all hours . . . and she has let down her hair and couldn't understand why her mother would desert her. Why her mother would not accept her as a child. And, ah, this she has never been able to clearly understand, and we have in our own way tried very very hard on numerous occasions to explain this . . . without too much success. Ah, I think she accepts the explanation and she realizes, I believe she realizes, that we're not lying to her, and that there's nothing we can do about it. But she will turn right around and say that she does not love us and she cannot love us because we are not her right parents. And this of course, ah, at its best is . . . pretty heartrendering and it's pretty hard to . . . for even a parent at . . . our age to sit down and try to, ah, resolve . . . and have an inner satisfaction. . . .

MOTHER: But back of all this she keeps telling us that "You can't make me do this, you can't make me do that. You are not my mother, you are not my father." Well, I feel that if she will accept us . . . I think things could be different. But it's that nonacceptance on her part. . . . And I don't know how we could try harder . . . I really don't . . . [very low voice] . . . because I'm open to suggestions. . . .

INTERVIEWER: You've tried as hard as you know how. . . .

MOTHER: I . . . we've tried everything. . . .

INTERVIEWER: Mmmhmm.

MOTHER: We've spanked, we've pleaded, we've cried, we've prayed, we've done everything . . . I don't know what else to do.

INTERVIEWER: Nothing seems to get beyond that barrier. . . .

MOTHER: [Slowly] Nothing . . . seems . . . nope . . . and always you get . . . thrown up . . . "You're not my . . . mother or father . . . I don't love you, I never have and I never will." [Sighs].

INTERVIEWER: That's a hard thing to hear.

MOTHER: It certainly is. Yup [long pause].

MOTHER: And then I think he was a little bit leery, too, in accepting us as parents, although he had been away from the father about two months, he had had opportunities of visiting him and certain things had been built up within him that he should do his job well . . . he shouldn't mind and he'll come back to him, you know, I love you, you know, and I want you. And you mustn't love anyone because it's going to be hard to leave.

INTERVIEWER: *This his father had been saying?*

MOTHER: Yes. At least that's [child's] words, now whether he actually did this because I think it was about a year, maybe a year and a half later, that [child] came to me and said, told me that, I just can't learn to love you, because I know that my father is coming for me, 'cause he had said that I'm going to keep looking and searching as long as I have breath within me. So I do believe that some of the things that [child] did and some of the things that [child] said could be traced back to the memory of the things that his father had said. "Don't mind. Be mean. Don't learn to love."

MOTHER: I think that he felt we took him away from his foster home and it was our doing, and it took a lot of doing to get over that resentment. Maybe he still feels something, I don't know.

FATHER: I think he would have been different if he hadn't been in quite so many foster homes before we got him.

MOTHER: They were always taking him away from something he loved. He said, "I loved her, I loved her." He'd say, "I hate you. I hate you, why did you take me away from there. I hate you." I said, "We didn't take you away," I said, "We wanted a boy like you and they told us . . . they had to take you to a permanent home." I think he's trying to retain . . . I don't know . . . it's just a feeling . . . that he's trying to retain his family, uh, you know, before we got him, and there isn't . . . he isn't going to allow anything else to get in there and disturb that little world he's living in, and that's what it appears.

In 29 per cent of the cases we felt the child had resolved the relationship to natural and foster parents with whom he had lived previously; in 35 per cent of the cases such ties were still latent but effectively handled, and in 5 per cent the problem was unresolved and such competitive allegiance was a source of conflict between child and adoptive parents; 20 per cent of the cases did not show enough information for a reliable decision on how the child was handling this problem.

COPING WITH MEMORIES

It should be noted that the foregoing categorization is static and applicable to the dominant pattern which seemed to emerge in the parents' discussion. Some mention needs to be made of the process of adjustment to past ties and memories. All of the children, even those who ultimately were regarded as having resolved this problem, had a period of transition—for some very short, a week or so, for some 3 to 6 months or longer —when they manifested a conflict of loyalty between former parents and siblings and their new families. During this time they spoke of their past experiences, asked questions about their parents, and tested the adoptive parents' acceptance of them by competitively alluding to other parents and the accomplishments of other parents. Gradually, however, for most of them the strength of present relationships began to assume priority in their thinking and feelings. The past began to recede, was less frequently referred to, less frequently recalled. The parents, equally anxious to forget there was a past, were allied with the child in a conspiracy to kill it.

By the time we came to interview these parents the past was, in most instances, a factor of no great significance in the relationship between the parents and children—at least, on an overt, conscious behavioral level.

As one parent said, it had been such a long time since they had talked about the memories the children had brought with them "that you don't realize these things are changing through the years until you sit down and talk about it."

MOTHER: *Well, I think that for the last two years or so, we almost forget that they're adopted or that they belonged anywhere else and now just sitting down and talking about it, I mean now that's* just bringing those things to our memory, I mean you finally get so you feel like you belong to one another and you forget about the past. I think that he's forgetting about the past actually because he doesn't bring anything up any more. It's been a long time now. I haven't even thought about these things for some time now until you asked about it.

FATHER: When they first, ah, when they first came they had very, very strong remembrances, they talked about it constantly. Of course that's all the life they had. It just gradually disappeared. After we had had them, oh, perhaps a couple of years we took a ride one Sunday and we went through the home town where they had been living and they didn't recognize. . . .

MOTHER: [Interrupting] . . . they didn't recognize it at all.

FATHER: They were playing in the back seat and looking out. . . .

MOTHER: [Interrupting] . . . "Oh, that's a nice looking house," and we said, "Does that look like anything you've ever seen?" "No, we've never seen that before. [Laughs.] We went right through the main street. It shows just how quickly a mind can take on new life if you just keep them busy . . . keep them happy. . . .

FATHER: Well, we never told them not to discuss this. We never interfered when they were remembering. . . .

FATHER: It kind of gradually fell off. I'll tell you, you know, uh, it was kind of a funny thing, you see, the evolution there. Well, when we first got him—and in fact, oh, golly . . . for a long time he, uh, really quite an imaginative child, and he told stories, oh, man, just fantastic tales, you know. . . . Of course we knew they were all figments of his imagination. But to begin with his brother was always in 'em. And it was always about events that had taken place on this farm. . . . Then gradually . . . as he was here longer and longer he was still talking about his brother, and he was still talking about events on the farm, except that we recognized the events as something that had happened to him around here. . . .

INTERVIEWER: I see.

FATHER: But he . . . he was still talking. . . .

MOTHER: *He was still keeping his old characters. . . .*

FATHER: *He was still thinking about the farm and about his brother but the events he was talking about were things that had happened to him since he was with us. And then, oh, I don't know, he just kind of gradually fell off.*

One of the more surprising adaptations to coping with the child's memories of earlier ties was to encourage the continuation of such ties. A general procedure in agency adoptions is that the adoptive family is insulated from contact with the child's natural family and with the child's foster family. Maintaining contact with some members of the child's original family as a procedure for helping the child to cope with memories of the past has some sanction in adoptive agency procedure. Schapiro notes that about 25 per cent of the agencies studied in a nationwide survey encourage the maintenance of past ties when placing older children (75, p. 31).

Bell reports:

Our agency has found great value in a process which, to many agencies, may represent a new departure in adoption—the preservation of the child's relationships with certain selected members of his natural family. Far from undermining the adoptive relationship, his keeping in touch with his relatives often strengthens it; the child knows that his adopting parents accept not only him but that which belongs to him and this acceptance has a broader, surer meaning (4, pp. 333–34).

Edwards (18) notes that visits by former foster parents to the child in his adoptive home has been helpful to the child in making the transition.

In 11 of our study group cases there were visits between the adoptive parents and the foster parents. In 2 other cases some contact was maintained by mail. In 10 instances there were visits between natural siblings in other homes and the adopted child in his home, and in 2 cases there were visits with grandparents. In 26 (28 per cent) different cases there was contact of some kind.

All such contacts were made subsequent to placement, most following legal adoption. In each instance the child's whereabouts were known to these people, all of whom played some significant part in the child's life prior to adoption. This is a confirmation of the disadvantage of older adoption cited by the parents—that the child is more recognizable and, prior to adoption, has had contact with more people who can possibly recognize him.

Older children can send and receive mail, know the addresses and whereabouts of relatives, and often remember telephone numbers, which they are capable of dialing. It is only with difficulty that parents can enforce a break in contact if the children wish to maintain it, and opposition is likely to arouse the child's resentment. Yet many of these contacts were arranged or passively accepted by the adoptive parents. By appealing to the agency these parents could have enforced a break, and some in the group did take steps to enlist the agency in preventing contact when it appeared imminent. In the 28 per cent of the cases where contact occurred the parents did not, apparently, take the steps available to them to prevent or end it.

MOTHER: . . . it didn't seem to bother me to take them to visit their grandparents . . . I thought it was . . . somebody that the children loved. Well, why shouldn't they, ah, go and see them . . . they loved their grandmother. . . . And we let them call at Christmas time . . . and by phone . . . and also at Easter time. They seem to, ah, feel so happy over hearing their voices . . . both the grandparents and the children . . . too . . . it affects [child] just a little bit yet . . . she kinda starts to cry a little bit . . . when she hears her grandmother's voice . . . probably it wasn't the best thing to do . . . but we felt so sorry for those old people . . . too . . . there was a love there . . . and it must have been an awful thing to just sit there and wonder, well, what part of the country are they in . . . what kind of a home are they in . . . so . . . we had them come and visit the children here . . .

and the grandfather said, he says, "Now we can go home and rest," he says, because he knew what kind of a home they had and that they were happy here, and then I was glad . . . that I did have the visits . . . but we didn't start with this level. The children had been here for some time and were, you know, pretty much settled.

FATHER: Well, this one family that has adopted the older sister . . . they brought her up here. They visit back and forth more or less . . . we can't say no or anything like that . . . it's O.K. with us.

MOTHER: Well, she knows that she had sisters . . . well, it wouldn't be quite right to say "You can't see 'em." I mean, because she already knew and was old enough to understand that . . . there were other children, I mean, there were more of her family. . . . And we felt she would maybe hold it against us if we didn't want her to associate with them so that, ah, we've never said anything against it. But then, we've never gone out of our way . . . too much to, you might say, to cement the ties closer than what they already are.

The contact is encouraged or permitted by the parents to help the child to deal with his memories in a way which assists his integration with the adoptive family.

MOTHER: And [child] expressed a desire to visit the foster home he had lived in for a long time. Then he had been here 2 years. We drove to the town where he had lived and walked down the road, and as we came to the particular house that I had decided might be the place, I said, "Does this look like the house to you?" Well, he wasn't sure, maybe, but he was a little hesitant. An older man came out of the garage and I said, "Is this the _____ residence? "Oh, they moved away a year ago." But I said, "Was this the place?" "Yes." And I said, "Well, would you mind if we walked around the yard. This boy lived with that family for a while and he'd like to see the place." "Go ahead." So we had a swing in the swing. The chicken house was empty and we walked around in that. We took some pictures out in front and then walked down

the road a little farther and there we found a boy named
B_____ that [child] had played with that summer. But
B_____ didn't remember [child] or was too shy to say any-
thing.

INTERVIEWER: What was the effect of all this on [child]?

MOTHER: I think it was a relief to him. I think it kind of cleaned up
something in his mind. I think he needed that. But I didn't want
to do it too soon; I felt that we had to wait until he . . . was
ready . . . it was very comfortable all the way around, and we
were glad that we did it. I don't know if we would have been so
happy if the family had still been there . . . but then, of course,
the situation might have been different. But as it was, he knew
that they were gone and he erased that from his mind and was
satisfied . . . and I guess in a sense it did the same for us.

MOTHER: He wanted to call his aunt every night . . . And I, ah,
I'd say, "Well, do you want to?" "Yes," he'd like to . . . well, I
found after the first week or so that . . . each time it got a little
shorter and shorter, there was a little less need to call her. And by
letting him do it, it worked itself out.

FATHER: Well, actually, when you look back on it though, I really
think that this was a way to help the children to find out if they
wanted to stay here.

MOTHER: . . . see, when they went back to the foster home the
first time they were still hostile when they came back to us, but
when they went the last time they didn't want any part of that
home any more and they wanted to come back here. . . .

Even though the parents accede to the child's desire for the
contact they are understandably somewhat anxious.

FATHER: We've been over there to the foster home. We went to
see them. I used to go fishing right next to it and I didn't even
know it. And so one day I'm going out there and I'm going
fishing, you know, and he kind of points and he says, "There's
where I used to live." I said, "Would you like to see it?" So I

took him back there, see, and he saw it and stuff, I just took him in to stop in and see it. . . .

MOTHER: Well, one time he wanted us to take him to visit them after he was adopted legally though. I must say I was . . . relieved that the adoption was final . . . so we did, and then when he was legally adopted. . . . he had some toys he wanted to give to the kids. . . . that he had outgrown . . . a little train . . . a building set . . . so he took them, for the older children to play with.

MOTHER: Keeping the memories alive they might build up the strength with the natural family and that's all right . . . but there's selfishness there again . . . adoptive parents sometimes say you shouldn't do that. . . . They don't want to share the child . . . with the natural parents . . . sometimes that's too hard for them . . . you know . . . when you love the child . . . it's kind of hard.

A frequent response of the parents' coping with the child's memories is to present themselves as open and receptive to whatever the child presents. This is in line with the approach advocated by the agency. The parents themselves were reluctant to initiate a discussion. "We never prompted him or asked him. It's just what he himself offered, never asked him any questions because we felt the less we talked about that the less he wanted to talk about it."

But once the child himself introduces this the parents made an effort to show active acceptance. The parents acted on the mental hygiene prescription that what is expressed and out in the open can be better handled and resolved than feelings hidden and unexpressed.

MOTHER: They would talk of their experiences, which we let them do. Whenever they wanted to talk, whatever they wanted to tell. We never told them, "Shhhh, don't say anything." If they wanted to, O.K. If it made them feel better, O.K., get it out of their systems. Get it out of their systems and then just forget it.

MOTHER: And I encouraged him to . . . tell anything even if it wasn't nice . . . [takes a breath] . . . because . . . when he talked about it . . . it got out so the wind could blow it away. It wouldn't stay inside and it couldn't hurt him . . . but if he kept things inside, either lies or truths, and . . . that bothered him . . . and didn't get them out . . . they would hurt him. I said, "You can tell me anything . . ." because I'm not going to hurt you for telling things that . . . whatever happened to you before you came here, you couldn't control very much, therefore you weren't very responsible for it. And of course I encouraged that so I would know what happened to him to help to . . . help to raise him.

MOTHER: Oh, for that first three months, we heard about that morning, noon, and night. And we listened with interest, we carried on this conversation about his farm as though we were really a part of it, or we'd just let him talk it out, get it out of his system . . . so I think our smart move was that we let him talk everything out about the farm and I mean, such simple things as the dump he would go on and play in, this big sand gravel place and now . . . well, then that conversation went on for, oh, then perhaps close to a year, but then it just kind of faded away, we don't even hear about it, haven't for. . . .

FATHER: Just gradually less and less, at first, I mean, he'd talk about it all day long, maybe you won't hear about it for a couple of days, and then a week, and then a month, and then it'd be two months. . . . I don't remember him saying anything about that farm in the last year. . . .

The child's references to former ties are accepted by parents in confidence that the phase will pass, that the child needs to go through this if he is to fully accept the adoptive parents. Confidence in the ultimate outcome gives the parents strength to make the most difficult of responses: not responding at all.

MOTHER: And gradually . . . it takes . . . it takes so much patience. It does get under . . . under your skin to hear this constant . . . the other father did this, the other mother did this, and you just get so fed up with it that, ah, I don't know, I'll admit I blew up several times, it just got so, I said, "I know but I've got to do things my way, it isn't going to be like the other mother did it." And, ah, it does take an awful lot of patience. With the older children.

FATHER: But if you have enough patience and stick with it, it gradually becomes less and less frequent. They finally forget all about it and you hear nothing more, then that's the end of it.

MOTHER: I'll tell you about something I think other parents may go through the same thing . . . and it was rather difficult for a little while but, ah, we got over this hurdle too . . . no matter what I would make, oh, maybe she was here five or six months, [child] would say, "Oh, my other mother made these so much better." And of course it was a period of letting it go, and, ah, I suppose and, ah, homesickness and wanting to have that other mother and dad in her own mind, and so I just used to feel so bad sometimes, it seemed no matter what I would make for her it just never was quite as good as her other mother . . . but finally she got over that . . . I remember one morning making hotcakes and she said, "Oh, my other mommy made much better hotcakes," and you know, I can just remember that because it made me feel so bad and I thought well, I just won't, I just won't say I bet your other mommy couldn't make better hotcakes and [laughing] . . . but if you go along with it, pretty soon it will just be in the background and forget it. . . . She wanted to cling to her background and no matter what I did it wasn't right . . . now if new adoptive parents go through this, some of them might become very discouraged and begin to fight back . . . there were times when I had a hard time keeping my patience. . . .

And sometimes a specific event, rather like an incisive interpretive comment made just at the strategic moment in psychotherapy, seems to focus psychic energies in resolving the conflict and in helping the parent and child to cope with the problem of memories.

MOTHER: *The only time he ever showed any emotion about his other family was the day we were to get our final papers, the day we were going to court. [Husband] called from work the day before and said, "Well, tomorrow's our big day." And so he said, "I think you better get his suit all pressed so that we can go out to dinner and so on," and so I was telling him all about it, and I tried to put everything on a comparison basis . . . you have a license to drive your car . . . and our dog has to have a license, and you know . . . really a license to buy your house, you know . . . everything on that comparison, and he seemed to understand and all, and we said that the judge would be all dressed up in his funny black robe and we would celebrate and go out to dinner. And that morning, I sent him on his way to school and I didn't hear the door close and I went out . . . and there he was with his little head on the counter in the kitchen and he was just sobbing, and I said, "Well, what's the matter . . . ?" "Nothing. . . ." I said, "Well, did I say something to hurt your feelings?" "No." "Did Daddy say something to hurt your feelings?" "Nope." And I said, "Well, can you tell me what's wrong?" "Nothing." So that was the one and only time in this whole deal that he broke down, and I said, "Well, come on, let's go in and sit down." And we sat in one of these chairs, and I put my arm around him and I said, "Well, now let's have a big cry." So he cried and I cried. It was pretty darn touching there, believe me, and so I said, "Well, now let's blow our noses and see if we'll feel better . . . now let's have a big long talk." I said, "Now, I know something's bothering you, and you know I've always told you everything if I could possibly tell you," and I said, "What's bothering you?" "Where are my brothers and sisters?" So I told him what I knew about his father and brothers and sisters. But the strange part of it is, he never once asked about his mother. And he knows his mother is alive, but that's the only time he ever came right out and asked about them. And he was kind of being a little stinker that day and then after we got done crying and that, I said, "Now, you don't feel so perky, I don't think we'll go to school, you're all red." So then I* said, "You go out and play in your sandbox," and I was painting the porch floor and he kept coming back to me and he'd say, "Mother, if I said no to the judge, that I didn't want to live here with you, what would you do with my sandbox?" And I said, "Well, maybe we'd give it to the kid down the block." Then it wouldn't be long and he'd be coming back with some other thing like that. He was just trying to needle me the whole day and finally I said, "I've gone along with you on this foolishness long enough. I think it's time, right now, that you and I are sitting down and having a serious talk about this." I said, "You just remember one thing, Daddy and I took an older child, because we wanted an older child, and we happen to have wanted a child with freckles, and we happen to have wanted a child with red hair, and you have it all," and I said, "You just remember that we wanted you." And I said, "You just know that that shoe goes both ways. Either you want us or we don't want it that way." And just then he said, "Well, mother, I've just been testing you all morning." He said, "You know I want you and Daddy for my mother and daddy." But you see, he was just feeling me out too. But I think, perhaps, the fact that we have both been so frank with him, no matter what he asked, if it's a good answer or not, he gets the truth.

These approaches to coping with the overt manifestations of the child's attachment to other parents take considerable ego strength on the part of the parents. Every such manifestation is a reminder of the adoptive nature of the relationship and a threat to the completeness of the child's love for the adoptive parent. There is recognition of what is implied by the expression of such memories.

FATHER: Once when she was recovering from an illness and was acting depressed I said, "Here you've got a beautiful room, you've got all sorts of things around you." We had a T.V. set and I said, "You should be happy that you're recovering from this illness instead of being depressed, what is it?" She said, "I once had a brother, a little tiny brother." I didn't know how to cope with the thing, I didn't know what to tell her. And finally I said, "You know there are things and events in our lives that have gone before . . . and we just have to more or less keep those memories because we cherish them, but let them become part of your life." But it bothered me, I felt a whole lot helpless, that's what bothered me . . . about it. I felt as though I had fallen down on the job some place . . . in my obligation to the child. I mean, some place along the line, I had . . . I felt as though I hadn't done what was proper. Because this thing had come out . . . I felt that we should have created surroundings in which she would be so completely happy that these past . . . was just a bunch of darkness, you see.

MOTHER: She had one aunt she was close to and wanted to visit. And I debated about this for a long time, what could I do? And I think I wasn't secure enough for her to go home, because I didn't feel like she belonged to us. Now I'd let her go any time she asked but now she doesn't ask. She hasn't for years.

MOTHER: Naturally, I think I do feel uncomfortable that they might want to locate their natural family . . . to the extent that I feel that sometimes children . . . think that the grass is greener on the other side, and that maybe if . . . they found their real parents maybe it would be a lot nicer than it is here . . . and I wouldn't ever want to go through that . . . I always say until they're 18, they'll stay here . . . and when they're 18 I'll be happy to give them their parents' name if they want to go back there and look them up; well, that's up to them.

Parents recognize the dangers to themselves, to the child, and to the relationship in active maintenance of such memories. The anxiety was expressed in a number of ways by the parents. Eight couples mentioned they had felt concern that the children might not accept and like them as much as they liked former parents. One parent said he wished the child had been in an institution rather than in a foster home because "the child would have no parents there at all, only advisors or counselors or something like that."

While the parents are gratified by the child's apparent forgetfulness of his earlier families they are also threatened by it. If the child's attachments are so shallow, will he not be equally likely to forget them?

MOTHER: *We tried to help him locate his brothers and sisters so they can write back and forth if it's too far a distance . . . or send pictures back and forth or something like that . . . just so he gets track of his family again some day, because I'm not afraid of losing him.*

INTERVIEWER: *That's not threatening to you?*

MOTHER: *Not a bit. Because I can tell how much love he has for his mother . . . he'll never stop loving her.*

The deprivation and suffering these children experienced at the hands of neglectful, indifferent and, on occasion, abusive, natural parents also assisted both the child and the adoptive parents in dealing with the problem. Young, in her study of neglectful, abusive parents, questions the claim that "children would rather be in their own home no matter how unhappy they may be. This was not the belief shared by many of the children in this study. . . . Grownups forget, or prefer to ignore, how realistic children are. They know their own weaknesses and cannot afford to be impractical" (93, p. 99). Children in our study were equally realistic.

They knew their best hope lay not in clinging to their natural family but in rejecting it in favor of the adoptive one. The agency records of these children report their reluctance to see the natural parents when they came to visit. One child, on a visit downtown with his foster parents, saw his mother and turned and went a different way so that he wouldn't have to meet her. Children were heard to say that they had better behave in the adoptive home, otherwise they would be sent back to their own mother.

FATHER: *Course, when he first got here and started tellin' us things about the way they treated him in his own home and in the foster home and everything like that, I said, "Well, gee, it's terrible"; why I said, "I wouldn't believe that people would treat children like that!" But I said, after having 'em . . . maybe it was a blessing in disguise that he was treated that way. It was that much easier for us to . . . to . . . fit him into our way of living. If he had been fondled and loved and cared for there, it would have been quite . . . it would have been a little harder to . . . break away, wouldn't it?*

For some children, then, their limited contact with their own parents made the problem of competitive ties less problematic for adoptive parents. In others the nature of the remembered relationship prompted the child to "work" harder at dissolving old relationships and cementing the new.

Name changes are associated with the problem of coping with past affective ties. Carrying the old family name symbolizes, and reinforces, identification with the family of origin. Acceptance of the adoptive family name, and the resolution of whatever emotional conflict this occasions, symbolizes the shift in identification and willingness to accept the new family.

A similar problem is involved in the readiness to accord the new parents the status titles to which they are entitled but which belonged, in earlier life, to the first parents. Children make a distinction in talking about an earlier life by referring to "my other father" or my "poor father" (as compared to the present, richer, father) or my "first mother," "my old mother" (as opposed to the "new" mother).

By the end of the first year all of the children had dropped their last name and were using that of adoptive parents without apparent conflict. All were using some form of parental title in addressing the adoptive parents—mom, dad, mama, papa. Such changes represented modifications in self-identification.

Some made such changes immediately upon coming to live in the adoptive home.

INTERVIEWER: *You said before that he didn't ask you how he should address you . . . he just started to call you Mom and*

Dad. What hesitancy, if any, did he show about accepting the surname for himself?

MOTHER: *That's what puzzles me; he dropped his own name right away. I don't think I could have done as well. He never mentioned that name and even when we see that same name around, he never says, "That was my name." He just dropped it without any hesitation; he never mentioned that name again and I'm sure that he has a vivid memory of everything, so that would not be just put out of his mind because he lost the memory of it . . . I don't think he's ever mentioned that name from the day he came.*

FATHER: *And right away when . . . of within twenty minutes after they got here . . . why . . . they, ah, asked me if I'd make 'em a toy gun . . . wooden gun . . . so we went out there in the shop and I was whittling out some wood, you know, and fixin' somepin' that looked some'eres near like a gun . . . and [child] says, "Mrs. Z_____ says we can call you daddy." And I says, "You sure can, if you want 'a." And by gosh from that minute on I've been daddy."*

INTERVIEWER: [To mother] *When did he start calling you Momma or Mother?*

MOTHER: [With difficulty] *Well it, ah . . . [child] didn't for . . . well, I imagine for three or four days . . . and then it was rather odd . . . [laughs] . . . we were in the car and the children were in the back seat . . . an' . . . he held his little wooden gun to my neck and says, "Stick 'em up, Mother." [Everybody laughs.] That was the first time and that kinda broke the ice, I guess.*

Some took a little longer.

INTERVIEWER: *What did she call you when she first came?*

MOTHER: *Hey! Wasn't it?*

FATHER: *Yah.*

MOTHER: *Hey, or hey you, or. . . .*

INTERVIEWER: *Uh huh. How long did that go on before she. . . ?*

MOTHER: *Oh, I don't know. Just like a couple of days wasn't it? Wasn't it R_____ or was it G_____ said, "I don't think that's very nice. I think we should call 'em momma and daddy,"* wasn't it? "I don't think it's very nice calling you hey," and they made that kind of decision on their own, I think, and he's been calling us Momma and Daddy ever since.

MOTHER: Well, I'll say right from the beginning, ah, she wouldn't call us Mother and Dad. And then she gradually did too . . . but I think it was hard for her, and I think she, ah, well, she was fighting this all the time, you know. . . .

Despite the difference in time which such changes required, by the time we came to interview the families in no instance were these matters a problem of current interest. In every case the transition had been made in terms of these outward forms of changed identification and allegiance.

Closely related to the problems of dealing with the child's memories of former living situations is the difficulty of dealing with the child's questions about his past. In some ways this is easier than in the case of infant adoption, since some of these children lived through the breakup of their family and were aware of it. Some had experienced their mother's illness and/or death, or her inability to care for them when a father deserted.

Yet in some other respects, answering the older child's questions about his family presents greater difficulties because the family situation which led to adoption of these children generally involved a rather prolonged period of social disorganization. Explanation is easiest in those cases which involved family tragedy—an accident or an illness, for instance, rather than family breakdown.

Some parents, knowing something about the child's family, were a little fearful of the hurt the child might sustain if his inquiries about his family were frankly answered. Others imply that the child, sensing some of this, protects himself by not inquiring. The parents were aware of the need to present the child with an acceptable picture of the natural parents, lest he —identifying with them—reject himself. Explanations were therefore given in terms of overwhelming circumstantial difficulties which made it impossible for the parents to care for the child—which, in its essential elements, is not far from the truth. Specific details were frequently unpalatable. Hence many parents either feigned ignorance of detail or deliberately cultivated ignorance about his background. Thirteen parents volunteered that they wanted only the limited information the agency shared with them. In addition to protecting them from uneasiness when the children raised questions, they felt that limited information permitted them a less prejudiced view of the children and allowed them to be less inclined to look for negatives in the child. The children, they felt, should be "taken for themselves, not for what their parents were." Not knowing, too, they were less inclined to worry about "what the child might turn into." As one mother commented," It's not good for yourself if you worry and wonder. . . . The more you do that, the less you're going to give to that child because you're going to start picking here and finding there and doubts here and doubts there . . . I don't think that's any good."

Some felt ignorance was helpful in contact with friends and relatives who inquired about the child's background. Here, too, honest ignorance prevented any extensive inquiry.

Some stated that providing limited information was deliberate agency policy so as not to discourage prospective adopters, and that this was agreeable to them. One parent said, "Perhaps if I knew all the details I would have chickened out," and he was glad that he had not been told. But avoiding knowledge of the child's early life conflicts with the need to be aware of this history so as to better understand him.

FATHER: *Probably not knowing all of the child's experiences, not knowing what experiences the child has had, as we said, earlier, makes it hard to understand him but I don't think I'd want to know. I would rather stay in the dark and feel my way, than to be told, to be briefed right down the line from everything that ever happened to the youngster, because if you knew some of the things that happened to her, you might want to go in there and choke somebody. And I don't have any feeling of animosity towards any of her people, anything like this, it was just an unfortunate experience and I'm willing to forget it. But I think that one of the handicaps with working with older children would be not knowing, but there again, I wouldn't want to know, so I mean it's a kind of a . . . dilemma.*

In the end what made the provision of limited information acceptable was the fact that most of these adoptions turned out well. In instances where there was difficulty the parents generally complained that the agency had not been frank enough with them, had not shared all they knew about potential difficulties, and that they should have been given more details.

The parents try to present a favorable picture of the natural parents in response to the child's questions, although the threat implied is recognized. One parent says, "Well, you know it's hard because I don't want to build these parents up to them so much that they would be better than we were, and yet I don't want to degrade them so much either because they are, after all, their parents."

The adoptive parent's readiness to accept the natural parent was based on an awareness that this is perceived by the child as an acceptance of himself. They recognize that they can best help the child to resolve his ties to the absent parents by accepting rather than opposing the child's feelings.

MOTHER: *When he started learning more in catechism in school, and you know how they teach children in catechism to pray for their parents and pray for their mothers, then once in a while he used to bring up his mother and I'd say, "Well [child] pray for her." I said, "She had you as a baby and don't ever stop loving her and pray for her." I just don't want to take his love for her away. Because that would be wrong, I think. Because when he gets older he would remember that, and he would look down on me for it. I don't want to take any of his love for his first mother away from him because then he is more satisfied and then he goes off and he doesn't think about it.*

Parents handle the questions that come up about the past very much in line with the current formula for sex education— only as much information as the child can understand and absorb in truthfully answering the questions they raise.

MOTHER: *I try to explain to 'em as much as I think they can soak up right now, you know. And then I told 'em as they get older I'll explain to them in more detail and I think they can understand it. I'm not going to tell them a whole lot that they aren't going to understand right now and then . . . would wonder about. I'm just going to tell them what I feel like they can understand at the time.*

Some of the parents have made notes of all of the information shared with them relative to the child's "own" family; they have sealed the material in an envelope and plan to share it with the child when he is older. In almost every instance when the child has raised the question, the parents have indicated their willingness to assist him in making contact with his own family when he is eighteen or twenty, if he should want to do this.

PATHOGENIC EXPERIENCES

One of the most frequently cited possible disadvantages of adopting the older child (given by 50 per cent of the parents), is that, having experienced physical and emotional deprivation and stress over a long period of time, there is a greater probability that the child will present some disturbed behavior.

MOTHER: *I have an idea that almost every child that's of that age, if you're going to move them . . . just moving them alone I think is going to cause some disturbance in their nature to some degree, it's going to have some effect on 'em . . . because you think back to your own childhood . . . when you were five or six years old and you've been moved out of your home into another home, it*

would certainly leave an effect on you . . . I can't imagine what
would have happened to me if something like that had ever been
done to me . . . so you can almost make up your mind what an
awful jolt that is to a five- or six-year-old mind . . . that maybe
hasn't been very secure to begin with. . . .

FATHER: Well, you've got to break down their resistance . . . to
believe in you, to trust . . . you . . . that's the biggest problem,
to make them trust you, because I imagine all children are the
same . . . it would be a pretty unusual youngster who did trust
anybody that came along after being pushed around . . . for that
many years.

Adoptive parents of older children have the problem, then, of
dealing with some of the psychological residuals of previous
pathogenic experiences. Given the lack, over a period of time,
in their childhood of a family group to which they securely
belonged, the neglect prior to separation from their own family,
the trauma of separation itself, and the uprootings and replacements which followed, one would expect some emotional disturbance in the child.

By far the most frequently encountered behavioral disturbance mentioned was enuresis; 17 children (19 per cent) manifested this over a long period—from 3–6 months to 5–6 years.
Except for 2 of the children, all had been "cured" and were no
longer enuretic by the time of the interviews.

Enuresis is a specific, objectively identifiable kind of behavior
which is annoying and upsetting to the parents. Other behavioral disturbances cited by the parents were similarly identifiable and upsetting to them. No other behavior was cited nearly
as frequently as enuresis. Five children had engaged in stealing
from stores or homes; 4 experienced nightmares and/or sleep-
walking with some consistency, 5 showed marked fear of the
dark, 2 were bed rockers, 4 masturbated openly and, in the
opinion of the parents, excessively, 3 were severe nail-biters, 2
truanted, 2 threw temper tantrums, 2 set fires, 1 manifested tics,
and 1 had engaged in some transvestite activity. Parents men-

tioned difficulty with less clearly defined symptoms such as lying, destructiveness, shyness and diffidence, "coldness," and "sibling rivalry."

Frequently parents mentioned the above behavior as having been manifested by the child for a short period of time after the child's movement into the home—"he did it maybe once or twice," "it happened for a couple of days," "after the first week he never did it again." These were not included in the above tabulation since they seemed normal concomitants to the problem of adjustment to the move.

Parents cited other kinds of behavior which created problems for them. These were not given any specific title but the description of the behavior manifested suggests problematic reactions to some of the experiences unique to the child facing substitute care. One suggests separation anxiety.

MOTHER: *Maybe he keeps worrying about what happened before, you know, because he'd been with us for about seven months . . . and I went to _____ for a funeral . . . and I discovered afterwards that [child]. . . .*

FATHER: *He was lost.*

MOTHER: *Yeah. And, ah, when they put me on the bus . . . why [husband] took the children to Sunday School . . . [heavy sigh] . . . and I found out, oh, some weeks later, that he cried through the entire hour.*

FATHER: *Sunday School.*

MOTHER: *And he cried many nights going to sleep . . . I was only gone the . . . little less than a week. . . .*

FATHER: *Four days . . . four or five days . . . [very low voice].*

MOTHER: *Five days, I guess . . . and, ah, there was a remark he made afterwards, that . . . his own mother left and never came back . . . so I felt bad to think I'd gone, but friends have told me maybe that was the best thing that ever happened to him because now he knows that I come back.*

INTERVIEWER: *He's actually tested it. . . .*

MOTHER: *Yes, but he was a very unhappy boy that week, I guess.*

MOTHER: And then I remember this . . . that there must have been something before . . . that bothered him because when he first came . . . he cried often and at night . . . he wanted me to go to bed with him . . . not to bed . . . but always with him. . . . And he'd always ask me if I'd go to some church circle or Scout meeting or something or even taking grandma up home to her house, he'd say, "Where are you going?" And, "When will you be back?" There was a little insecurity . . . at first. I didn't like to leave him and then I'd be . . . assure him . . . that everything was fine and that he was all right.

MOTHER: I discovered that when [child] knew that . . . that the welfare worker was coming here to visit her, little as she was, I didn't realize this at first but after this happened a few times I began to realize that she was so afraid of being taken away from here . . . that she would get up earlier in the morning than ever, a day or two before when she thought the social worker was coming . . . she would clean the bathroom, fix it up, and clean up her room, she'd do anything that she could as young as she was . . . because she wanted us to have something good to say about her. . . . This really made me sad.

FATHER: But you get in a large crowd like that at the ball game, he's still afraid that I might just accidentally go to the rest room . . . he's constantly got to have his eye on me. . . . He'd want a coke and then we'd have to wait in line because of the big crowds and I got tired of waiting in line and I told him I'd sit there, I'd give him the change, "You go get it," and he wouldn't do that at all . . . because I'd be between him and another man, you see, so I don't know how long this will last, if it's 21 or 41 or forever . . . because he has that feeling of . . . and I don't know how in the world to break him of that. . . .

MOTHER: She had never been back to [city where she lived as foster child] until this summer. And we took her with us one day and I kept saying, "[Child] are you carsick?" She sat there just with the most awful look on her face, it made me just sick. I said, "Do you suppose she wants to go back?" And that was it, because *we went shopping and came home and all the way home she just giggled and laughed. . . .*

FATHER: *As soon as we got in the car and headed for home. She was altogether different. And then we could actually realize that . . . we kind of figured that maybe they thought that we were taking her back. . . .*

MOTHER: *This is something else older children realize too. When we first adopted the children and if we would have company come in, if I would say "Now this is Mr. and Mrs. So and So coming," that was fine, they anticipated it, but if we would have drop-ins, especially if they were dressed up, if the man had on a white shirt, those kids would disappear so fast, you know, I think they thought they were being looked over again. They were ready to go out again. And they just wouldn't show their faces.*

These children had experienced separation and were aware that it might happen again. They demonstrated in their behavior their anxiety about this and attempted to defend themselves against such a calamity. There is then a greater sensitivity to the anxiety provoking aspects of any kind of separation from the parents.

They demonstrated mistrust and insecurity, too, as a result of previous experiences which had taught them that adults could not be trusted. Rejection was more than an academic word for them. It was not for them a fantasy to be feared but an actuality which might be repeated.

MOTHER: *It would get you; it was pitiful and everything to see how the boy, no matter what he was doing—why, eating or anything —he'd watch . . . really like an animal would. Alert. On the alert. Always watching. And of course he did tell me that this summer. Oh, we had a heart-to-heart talk and he said, "Well, you just don't trust anybody." He never trusted anybody until now— and it comes even now slowly.*

FATHER: *Well, I don't know what [wife] would think but I would say the hardest thing was the breaking down of that resistance*

. . . that outer shell she had . . . her determination not to like us. To try to win her over . . . to try to win her affection . . . because it was, ah, it was a big problem . . . I know she made the remark to the welfare worker . . . I think . . . but she said she was going to be real mean and she would have to take her back to the foster home . . . and she tried not to like us. For instance, it was after Christmas, because we'd given her a lovely Christmas, and she came out and she said, "Oh, I've never seen anything like it." So we thought well, that's the turning point. And, ah, very quickly she thought, ah, she forgot herself . . . and she said, "Ah, it was nothing." She later said to me, "Well, you can't blame me for not liking you and loving you." I said, "No, I don't blame you." She says this now as she looks back . . . she's a very smart little girl . . . and, ah, she said "You just don't trust people, momma," I said, "I realize that. . . . I don't blame you." She's a very affectionate girl now . . . very affectionate . . . but it took her a year and then one night she reached up and she said, "I love you."

FATHER: I don't know what he was thinking. I think he had probably been rejected so much that he was, uh, used to change, and I don't expect he was really ready for anything. I think he was simply a little boy that had been kicked around all over the place, and I think he'd been in so many other places that coming with us, I doubt that the fact that he was told that he might be adopted meant anything very much to him really.

MOTHER: He was just so . . . artificially good for so long. Because he was so afraid . . . that we wouldn't . . . adopt him. He had been disappointed so often before he couldn't believe anything.

Other children demonstrated behavior which suggested a deprivation of affectional needs earlier in life and a regression to earlier developmental levels in an effort to meet this deprivation. They had missed part of their childhood and sought opportunities to seek the gratifying affection which had been withheld and denied.

MOTHER: When he was here about the third year . . . [takes a breath] . . . he said, "You know mother, I wish instead of being

in all them houses, that you had been right there, the minute I
was born . . . and picked me right up and taken me home." So
he was telling me that to be in all of those houses, to have the
background that he had . . . and to come into a new situation at
his age . . . was very hard for him and he wanted to start from
the beginning with me and he did that . . . he would crawl up in
my lap . . . like he wanted to be cuddled and snuggled . . . and
he'd, ah, press against me . . . I'd give him a good hug . . . and
. . . then that was enough, he'd run out and play. If friends were
here—he'd always do it, in fact, in front of somebody . . . as
much as to say . . . this is my mother. . . . She belongs to me.
And you're here but she's my mother . . . and she belongs to
me. . . . You're just a friend, and in fact you're a little bit
out. . . . She's mine . . . and, ah, when he'd go out, they'd say,
"Look, doesn't it embarrass you to have that big boy crawl up in
your lap and act like a baby?" I said, "No." I knew why, and I
didn't feel called upon to explain it to them. . . .

MOTHER: Our little girl was three at the time that [older child]
came to live with us, and I was rocking her occasionally and he
couldn't get over it, he said that I was rocking her. It apparently
seemed that he had never experienced being rocked, so then I
rocked him. Well, he was almost five years old, and you could tell
that he had never experienced anything like this. So, he, I guess
he must have had quite a bad life before. He must not have had
the affection he should've at those years, and I think that has
shown in him.

MOTHER: He used to talk baby talk when we first got him. This
kind of seemed funny for a seven-year-old boy. But he did. He
talked baby talk. He'd say mommeeee [soft voice,] you know.
He'd say, "Come here, mommmeeee." He just didn't have what
he needed when we got him.

FATHER: I mean in his infant ways, you knew he hadn't had enough
. . . fondling in his infancy.
MOTHER: He was still a little baby. I mean, he wanted loving. My
brother's daughter had an old beat-up doll . . . and he wanted
that doll. She was all rags and, I mean, the insides were out, but

he wanted that doll to go to bed with him and that was fine [voice speeds up]. And then finally she parted company completely and then I said, "Well, I'll buy . . . I'll go get you another doll." Well, that must have been two years after we had him, or three years. Two years at least, and I said, "I'll go and get you another doll." "But don't tell the clerk, momma, that it's for me." You know, he wanted something to put his affection on, but he didn't want anybody else to know about it. So then I bought him a teddy bear and he had that for about a year that he went to bed with.

FATHER: Well, when we first got her she couldn't cry. I got her roller skates, the rest of the kids had roller skates and she fell down, learning to roller-skate. She fell on her butt and, uh, she'd just try holding it back, you know. And I said, "Cry." I said, "It hurts, don't it?" I said, "Do you feel like crying?" She says, "Mmm." I said, "Go ahead and cry." And you should have heard her cry.

MOTHER: She really let loose.

FATHER: And then that caused a little problem then for she'd cry for everything. Well, she found out she could cry . . . she made up for crying, for all the years of not crying. . . . Then afterwards the kids said, "Well, crybaby." Now she cries if she has a reason, if she hasn't a reason she don't cry. But, she found out that she didn't have to restrain it.

Indiscriminate, shallow manifestations of affection are, like lack of affect, another response to early deprivation. A few of the adoptive parents noted this reaction: the children, as though starved for affection, sought it indiscriminately and constantly.

MOTHER: But the thing that worried me the most was when they went to school that people . . . they loved people . . . so they were so hungry for love and attention that any car that would stop. . . . And I talked and I warned them and I would . . . every time anything that happened that would be on the radio or in the paper I would go over it and over it with them and read it to them over and over what happened to this child just because it was offered a ride, got in the car, and that was it.

MOTHER: Well, ah, when we first got him I could see that he wanted, oh, he wanted to be loved so much, and that hurt me a lot, to think that he had missed a lot of loving as a young child, and he knew that because, oh, he always wanted to sit on my lap and well, even now when he goes to bed he always comes and says good night and kisses us on the cheek, but when we first got him we could see that he was just desperate for love, he had missed out on that for some years, and that's what made me feel so bad . . . a lot of times I wished that I could have had him when he was younger, you know, cuddled him more and loved him more, but we tried to make that up . . . you know that he had lost . . . showed him a lot of love . . . all that we could give him you know . . . and still we didn't want to overdo it, either, and . . . [laughs] . . . so that we'd spoil him you know. . . .

Having been disappointed before, and having had their first tentative manifestations of trust abused, some of the children needed reiterated and repeated assurance that the adoptive parents wanted them and loved them.

MOTHER: She didn't know what it was to be loved. She would cuddle up and want to have an arm around her while watching television. My sister-in-law, that first Christmas, asked her, "What do you want for Christmas?" And she said, "Love." At six years old. That's quite something, quite something.

MOTHER: He wasn't as well liked as the foster parents' own child, and he was jealous of the foster parents' child R_____ and I would reiterate how much we loved him and he said, would say, "Do you like me better than R_____?" and I said, "Well, I don't even know R_____, but I like you. I'm sure I like you better than R_____." He needed that reassurance, feeling that he was first place in this household at least. And I remember when he first came, course the telephone was ringing constantly, people would call up to . . . when they had heard the news and [child] *would just stand around and listen, and he'd say, "Tell them . . . how glad you are." And he wanted me to tell, if I didn't say it fast enough. . . .*

Because of the child's fear and mistrust, adoptive parents of older children need the patience and self-confidence which permits them to move at the child's somewhat slower pace in reciprocating affection.

FATHER: *You don't push yourself, if they come to you fine and dandy. If they don't, well, you wait. When a child gets to know you then they'll come. I use the same principle with her. I figured, O.K., honey, you'll come whenever you get ready. You find out I'm not gonna hurt you then, uh, those things are hard . . . I don't blame her. It was a good six to eight months before she backed herself up and sat on my lap over in the corner.*
MOTHER: *I said to him, I said, "Don't push."*
FATHER: *You couldn't rush, couldn't rush.*
MOTHER: *Don't push, it's just that it'll come, it'll take time.*

MOTHER: *It took him almost a year before he could show affection. Well, that's where you're going to wait . . . with an older child you have to wait for him to come around. You can't force yourself onto that child.*

The parents try to give the child what he needs, and yet in some instances he is incapable of accepting what they offer. A benign therapeutic environment appears to be an insufficient corrective in developing the child's capacity to respond.

MOTHER: *He was always, uh, what is this—he was testing us out. How much did he need to convince him that we cared?*
FATHER: *Well, I feel that you can just give so much of yourself. Then there has to be some giving back.*

MOTHER: *Now how're you going to dish it out enough . . . of any certain thing to give him what he needs? I don't know. . . . You* just can't hug him all the time. He's so far behind on love that it just can't catch up with him. And how do you give him enough? You can, uh, if somebody's short of sugar you can give them a whole lot, and the body will take it, you know, giving you an example. But how can you give him enough affection, inside of a boy, to help him. You can't do it.

MOTHER: Uh, of course your patience lasts only so long too, I think. For the first year I had all the patience . . . in the world and then even for the, the next, maybe the second year, when he was rebelling so openly. . . . And you keep giving patience and more patience until the . . . time comes when you don't have it. It's gone and, uh, like I remember one time he said, "Remember how nice you were to me when I first came." He said, "You used to like me, didn't you?" Well, of course he had, uh, I had to assure him that I liked him fine right now. But there comes a time when you just . . . saying the same thing after a while you just can't say it sincerely . . . as I say, you're human.

Parents tried to accomplish the difficult task by taking it easy and letting the children know in many ways that they really belonged.

FATHER: I think that security was probably the thing that they were . . . what they were looking for, that they had never been able to feel that—not what you could count on . . . that you could kind of sense in them that they had never had any security.

INTERVIEWER: How did you help them to feel secure?

FATHER: Well, by just letting them know that they were part of the home, that. . . .

MOTHER: [Interrupting] . . . that we loved them both.

FATHER: We loved them and they could pretty well do what they pleased as long as they stayed . . . reasonable. I mean they could go outside, and if they wanted to come in and get something out of the refrigerator to eat, I mean, go ahead, if you're hungry, come in and if you want a slice of bread get it. . . . And, ah, I think those are all things that make them feel more like they're part of the household . . . and the family.

The parents recognized that by virtue of what they represented, coupled with the child's previous experience with parents, they excited a negative transference in the child; this acted as a barrier to the establishment of a positive relationship. In 9 instances the parents indicated an explicit awareness of this.

FATHER: *He's more considerate of me than he is of* [the mother].

MOTHER: *I think, well, that's probably just because he's taking his spite out on me because of the way his own mother must have treated him. But he's not nearly as respectful of me as he is of* [husband]. *He just plain ignores me a lot of times when I ask him to do something, but* [husband] *often asks him to do the same thing and he'll do it.*

MOTHER: *A lot of times adopted . . . children, well, they kind of hate their parents, you know. I mean, ah, I mean the adoptive parents . . . maybe as a resentment because their own parents didn't keep them or something . . . you know . . . and they go against them . . . not knowing, without understanding why they're doing it.*

MOTHER: *Well, she was with her, with her mother, until she was about seven I think, six or seven. And she transferred her mother hatred from her original mother . . . to me. And I had an awful problem.*

Theoretically, one of the principal conflicts for the child in adoption lies in the fact that he has, in reality, two sets of parents. The child who has never known a change in parentage splits the image of his parents into the two components to match the normal ambivalence felt for parents, the image of the good parent—congruent with positive ambivalence—who is the source of gratification, pleasure, rewards, and so forth, and the bad parent—congruent with the negative component of his ambivalence—who punishes, disciplines, frustrates, and denies the child. However, since the same parent both gratifies and punishes, the child is forced to resolve the fantasy and accept both the attractive and hateful aspects of the same parent figure. It is said that the adoptive child can invest each of his sets of parents with a different aspect of his ambivalence. As a result, the absent parent can be idealized.

Since the absent parent never punishes or disciplines, it is easy to see him as all loving, all gratifying. This formulation is suggested by Schechter (74, p. 29). However, an explicit examination of adoptive childrens' fantasies found this true of only 11 per cent of 35 adoptive children receiving private psychiatric treatment in Chicago (3, p. 41). Krugman found such fantasies in only a few of the psychological test records of 50 children with whom, as a psychologist, she was familiar (42, p. 355). In only 2 cases did it appear that the children in this group presented such a picture of their relationship, in fantasy, to their own parents. One parent presents this picture of the child's reaction in almost classical terms.

FATHER: *She talked about her mother. Ah, she remembers her mother as the person who came to see her on Sundays, who always brought a gift. . . . Who always combed her hair . . . who was the charming person . . . she hasn't remembered her now for, oh, many, many years . . . she doesn't remember . . . this at all any more, but at that time . . . everything that was unpleasant with us was an unfavorable comparison to the mother . . . who she saw . . . once, ah, once a week, if that often. Her mother had never had any . . . hand at disciplining her, she'd only brought her presents and combed her hair and . . . been nice to her. So this was an ideal fairy that comes . . . and of course we suffered a little bit in comparison there because we'd have to do things. We had to make her eat her vegetables, and we had to cut out the chocolate because of her teeth. We had to make her drink her milk. She doesn't mention her mother now . . . for . . . oh, gosh, she hasn't mentioned her mother for six or seven years. She says nothing.*

At some time or another within the first 2 years after placement, 8 adoptive couples faced some major disagreement with the child as a result of which the child threatened to run away. With surprising unanimity 7 of these couples faced the crisis by volunteering to help the child pack—by facing him, in fact, with the consequences of his threat. In effect they took advantage of the child's dependency. In consequence they may have engendered some unexpressed hostility in response to the child's frustration, as well as exciting fears of rejection and abandonment. Nevertheless, in each case the crisis was resolved —and the parents felt, on a pragmatic basis, that the approach was effective.

MOTHER: *Well, he didn't want to eat it. So then he'd been using this all the time, "You don't love me." You know, and I'd always assure him and say, "Well, honey, we love you a lot or you wouldn't have been here." And I thought, well, I'm not going to say that. So when he said, "I know why you want me to eat that old chili, it's cause you don't love me." And I said, "Do you know something, you're right." [laughing] He had been here a year then, it was just before Valentine's Day. I felt then that he should be feeling that he is wanted and loved and get over this little crutch that he was carrying that I didn't think he should continue. . . . So he said if that's the way we felt he was going to leave. And I said, "Fine, I'll help you pack." Well, he didn't want my help, and after he put some things in his bag he started uptown and my husband said, "Let him go. I think that all children have to go through this." So, ah, I said, "Well, you'd better let me know where you're going because I want to send you valentines when they come." So I know it was a day or so before, see? And he started out with a suitcase I got for Christmas and we were biting our noses to spite our faces because he dragged [laughing] it all the way to the corner. And [husband] went up there, he followed him with the car, so he waved and said, "Hi, Dad, where you goin'?" [Husband] said, "I'm going to _____, where are you going?" He said, "Gosh, I don't know, do you suppose Mom misses me?" So he said, "Gee, I don't know, I think you'd better go and find out for yourself." So he ran all the way home, you know, and then he said, "Did you miss* me?" And I said, "Oh, that little boy that left here, I wouldn't give two cents for him, but oh, I do love you." So that solved it, you know [laughs].

MOTHER: I remember one time too when he pulled a little trick on me; he was gonna go back, 'cause I had disciplined him. . . . "Yep, I'm going back." I said, "That's all right. If you want to go, just go upstairs and pack your things and you can go." "You go pack them." "No . . . if you want to go, you just go upstairs and pack your things," I said, "I'll put a basket there for you, and you can pack them and you can go." "Well, first you have to call up, Ma." I said, "No, we don't have to call up. We'll just . . . just take you, if . . . you want to go." He never went as far as the door to pack his things [in a choked voice]. I said, well about that time, if I would've put on a little act and said, "Oh, we don't want you to go, oh F_____, no, no," then he would have held that over my head all the time.

INTERVIEWER: Yeah [pause].

MOTHER: O.K., go. I knew he wouldn't.

These behaviors are grounded in the child's developmental history and activated by the adoptive situation. All are more likely to be manifested by the older adoptive child than by the adoptive infant, who has not experienced deprivation, rejection, and separation, and who has not—in consequence of these traumatizing experiences—developed the anxieties, hostilities, mistrust, and negative expectations which make emotional sense of the behavior of these children. These behaviors present problems for the adoptive parent of the older child and constitute additional disadvantages of adopting older children.

The fact that several of these children manifested some of these behaviors might support a contention that all of the group share the feelings which result in such behavior. To argue for or against such a statement is speculative. Many of the families, as far as we know, based on the parents' perceptivity and willingness to share, did not encounter difficult behavioral disorders, separation anxiety, mistrust, regression, or negative transference. None of these specific behaviors were manifested, according to the parents, by more than 20 per cent of the group.

It might still be well for parents and social workers to be sensitive to the possibilities that such behavioral difficulties may develop. However, it would be incorrect to anticipate the likelihood of such behavior in every case, or even in most cases of older children in adoption.

A second proviso is that even when such behavior was manifested it did not mean the breakdown of the placement. In some cases these difficulties did make satisfaction in the relationship impossible for the parents and, hence, for the child. In many other instances this was another problem to be solved and the parents did, in fact, resolve the difficulty. Children were healed; behavior changed, mistrust was dissolved, and permitted regression was given up. With the parents' patience, humor, firmness in guidance, and assurance of love and acceptance the problems were found to be surmountable. The adoptive home did the work of therapy.

To recapitulate, while such problems may be encountered by any adoptive parents of older children, they were in fact encountered by a limited number. But, even when actually encountered, in many cases they proved amenable to solution and susceptible to resolution.

Disciplining the child is a significant aspect of the role of the parent, who is called upon to socialize the child to the ways of the group by explicit education, identification with parental behavior, positive rewards for conforming behavior, and so on. Inevitably, certain occasions call for negative sanctions and punishments. Discipline is a problem for all parents partly because a variety of, often contrary, disciplinary approaches are recommended by experts.

Most of the adoptive parents faced with this problem used a combination of disciplinary techniques. Some "talked" to the children, some withheld privileges and affection, some scolded and nagged, some spanked. It is interesting to see that spanking is admitted as disciplinary procedure when one remembers that these parents had unanimously expressed disapproval of spanking during the adoptive study.

FATHER: *I shouldn't maybe tell this, but she can aggravate you . . . just till you're beside yourself . . . you almost lose control of yourself . . . it's just impossible . . . and I've gotten real angry at her and I've taken her to her room . . . and taken a belt . . . and whacked her over the fanny with it . . . and one good whack over the fanny and she'll just settle down as nice and calm as you please.*

MOTHER: *And you know, we . . . we were not old hands at raising children . . . of course, we told everybody else how they were supposed to raise theirs [laughs] before we got him. But, uh, we didn't know just how far you, you should go along with the youngster. . . . I remember the first day that I ever spanked him, [husband] was out in the office . . . and, oh, it was several things, he wanted to go over to S———'s and play, and it was about eleven thirty and I said, "No, you can't go because you're going to eat pretty soon," well, then he was mad and then he said, "Well I'm going to eat right now." I said, "No, no. You wait until Dad comes in," then he was mad. . . . And I just reached a point and I just waited . . . and I called [husband] out at the office and I says, "You've got to come in, I just spanked [child]." He says, "Where is he?" and I said, "He's in the bathroom crying." I got the dinner on the table and we sat down and he's still in there and he's crying and [husband] says, "H———— you better come on out and eat now." So pretty quick he came out . . . he sort of sidled around the door, you know, and came over and sat down . . . and he said he was sorry. And then we ate and that was it, you know, everything was all cleared up. Afterwards when I thought, now why did I spank that kid, I remember, it was . . . I could see it was all these things building up until finally you just had to knock him down. . . .*

INTERVIEWER: Um hmm. At the time it seemed the right thing to do.

MOTHER: *It just seemed like the only thing.*

In addition to choice of technique of discipline there are problems about its aims and limits.

FATHER: . . . like I've said a lot of times, you know when raising kids you've got to draw an awful line . . . a very fine line . . . I mean, you don't want to lick a kid until he doesn't have any gumption left, uh, and yet you don't want him to have such a temper that you know that he can't control himself. . . .

But whatever disciplinary technique is used, toward whatever end, a good feeling is generally manifested by these parents toward the children. There is clearly apparent in the interview material a desire to understand, a desire to be helpful, a desire to do right by the children. Reading the typescripts and/or listening to the tapes rarely evokes the feeling that these are essentially hurtful people who used discipline to satisfy their own needs rather than to further the interests of the child.

MOTHER: [Laughs] I thought the other night that maybe I'd been too rough on him . . . he was helping me set the table . . . like I said, and we had, uh, spaghetti and meatballs . . . and he put two plates on the table and he was coming over with a third, and I don't know if it got hot on the bottom or not but he just sort of spilled out about half of it on the table . . . and, well, we voiced our displeasure . . . but anyway it happened and, well, we forgot about it . . . and sat down and ate, then the next morning he was going to go up to the fair with H_____ early, and I was supposed to wake him up . . . so I woke him up. . . . He sat up in the bed and said, "What did I do? What did I do?" [Laughs]
FATHER: So then we got to thinkin' maybe we'd been too mean. . . .
MOTHER: Poor little guy. . . .

The fact of adoption complicates the task of discipline for the adoptive parent. This is particularly true for the adoptive parent of the older child. Unlike the parent who adopts an infant, adoptive parents of the older child face the problem of discipline almost immediately. Some activities need to be discouraged; some behavior needs to be changed. And discipline needs to be initiated without the advantage of knowledge about and experience with the child's pattern of response to the variety of disciplinary procedures available. Parents who adopt infants are not immediately called upon to "discipline" the child. When this problem has to be faced they have, over time, developed some knowledge of what procedures are likely to be effective with their particular child.

MOTHER: *I think that's what got on my nerves the most, because just all of a sudden it was there, the fighting and the quarreling, you know. Like with your own from little up why, I think you just gradually work into it probably, but all of a sudden—oh, dear, at the end of the day I was ready to tear my hair sometimes. . . .*

Parents tend to be empirical and pragmatic in their disciplinary approaches. They have to be. They measure the effectiveness of any approach by the actual results and make changes accordingly. The parent who knows a child from its infancy has learned on the basis of long trial and error which approach gets optimum results; he has learned to individualize discipline. The adoptive parent of the older child has to learn all of this quickly, while actually involved in major disciplinary problems.

MOTHER: [Sigh] *This is really an experience. I've often said I wish I could just write a book about [child]. When we first got him, too, he was always on the defensive. Always. And it didn't do us any good to spank him. "Hit me, see if I care." So I said, well, that isn't doing me any good; I'll have to try a different approach. So then, I would sort of sit in front of him and say, "Why did you do this?" "Nobody wants me, this is just like in _____." And the tears would just roll down his little face. "Nobody cares about me." [Voice mimicking a whine.]*

FATHER: *But if you wanted to spank him or anything, you couldn't draw a tear out of 'em [pause]. I suppose he'd had so many spankings that he's callous to it. Didn't mean a thing to him . . . spanking didn't bother him. None of it.*

We noted above that the adoptive parents of the older child face the problem of winning acceptance from a child who is in a position to give or withhold, to make favorable or unfavorable comparisons with other parents he has known. The anxiety some parents feel about their acceptability to the child makes them hesitant in disciplining. One needs to accept the risks of a negative reaction—anger, resentment, rejection, etc.

A positive relationship is the anodyne which makes discipline acceptable. The parent of the older adoptive child has to build a positive relationship and discipline at the same time.

FATHER: *It is a real rough row to hoe . . . when you bring a child in that big; and I mean you gotta have discipline, you gotta discipline 'em, and still you've gotta love 'em. You gotta make them love you and still you got to make them know the difference between right and wrong, at the same time . . . [pause].*

The child's past stands in the way of disciplinary measures in the present. Parents know these children have suffered in the past, and they hesitate to deny a child who has been so often denied. This stays their hand in discipline and makes them less spontaneous in reaction to the child.

Parents realize too that because of past negative experiences these children may be emotionally damaged. Consequently they may not feel ready to apply the usual run of disciplinary measures in the usual way, since the effect on these children may be different.

MOTHER: *I said that three years ago if anyone could have told me that I'd punish a child or be as firm with a child as I have been* with these, I would have said you don't know what you're talking about. But I thought it was the only way. You just couldn't, you just can't . . . cannot treat an adopted child, an older child, like you would a child that . . . in a normal home. Brought up in a normal home . . . you really and truly can't.

The older child has typically experienced inconsistency in discipline as he has moved from home to home. If inconsistency makes it more difficult for the child to build a stable, coherent superego, then these children are likely to present more than an ordinarily difficult task for the adoptive parents. The content of discipline may even have varied—behavior forbidden in one home may have been more accepted in another.

These children may also present difficulty because they have known diffuse sources of authority. At one time their natural parents were the source; with termination of parental rights it was assumed by the agency. But while in the picture, the agency did not itself administer discipline. Foster parents could not do certain things to the child without agency permission. The source of authority was not sharply defined, not sharply focused for the child. This experience with diffused disciplinary authority encourages the cry of many adoptive children: "You have no right to punish, you're not my real parents."

The older child, having had prolonged contact with natural parent and with diffuse authority, may be even less willing than most adoptive children to award the adoptive parents exclusive entitlement to disciplinary authority.

MOTHER: He came home very late and I was worried, and I said, "If you're smart, you'll just be real quiet . . . just waltz you right along upstairs mister." Well, then he went upstairs and slammed the door and was just as belligerent as he knew how, you know, so I started to read the paper. Well, one thing about him, he does think things over, you know, and he'll come around your way, which is a wonderful thing, I think, in his behalf, well, anyway, he said, ah, he said, "Mom, can I come downstairs and talk to you?" And I said, "Well, if you have anything constructive to say, I'm all e rs." So he came down and he said, "Well, I'm sorry that I came home so late but," he said, "you know some of the other kids said, 'Why do you have to go home? You don't have to listen to her, she's not your mother.' " And I said, "Perhaps I'm not your mother but I do want to be."

FATHER: *Especially when you're adopting older children . . . I think that you've always got the thing in the back . . . in the back of their minds anyhow that you aren't their real parents and, uh, I think that's quite a handicap. . . . Especially if their ideas don't agree with yours . . . there are many . . . things that they want to do, uh, you don't approve of well, then of course, you're just all wrong. . . . If anything comes up that, uh, we talk to 'em about seriously . . . well, you just adopted us . . . you aren't our real parents . . . and, uh, they'll say that . . . that it shouldn't count or something like that. . . .*

Adoption complicates discipline for some parents because they feel they are under the scrutiny of the community even though this may not be objectively true. Hence they feel they need to take community reaction into consideration in disciplining the child. Frequently, discipline has to be administered to older children under the eyes of the community, rather than in the privacy of one's home. The effects of unsuccessful disciplinary efforts are visible to the community as the older child, unlike the infant adoptee, displays his behavior in school, the playground, and local stores. Parents felt that they were perceived as acting for the community in caring for these children and were, consequently, answerable to the community for the kind of care.

MOTHER: *People who adopt children, somebody is always spying on them, the townspeople are always calling you and telling you what you should do about your children stepping in mud puddles [laughs], and their children can be drowning in mud puddles and that's all right . . . that's nobody's business . . . but when you adopt a child. . . .*

FATHER: *Everybody wants to be in on it.*

MOTHER: *I feel that I was overly conscientious about doing a good job . . . [laughs]. And, uh, I think a lot of people probably look around and they'll watch an adopted child closer to see if anything's cropping up! I think they watch more closely to see if they're well taken care of, or if they're dressed well . . . I think if you adopt I think they watch you a little bit closer to see . . . how good you're doing . . . you know, I think that way you're more on a . . . judgment seat.*

In retrospect the parents felt that they should have been firm sooner in disciplining. In saying this some noted that this is not so much a difference between adoptive and nonadoptive parents but rather a difference between experienced and inexperienced parents. They felt that parents generally capitalize on their experience with the first child and tend to be firmer with the second child.

It is difficult to generalize from the actions of these parents, since there were so many variations in the age and previous experience of the children and the family context into which they moved. One precarious generalization may, however, be ventured. With due regard for the needs of the child, disciplining the older adoptive child may be easiest if the fact of adoption is muted and the child treated as fully one's own. The counterpart of the child's rejection of the parents' right to discipline is ambivalence of the parent about his right to discipline the child. The less ambivalence there is about such entitlement the more limited is the conflict in application of discipline.

MOTHER: *I tried to treat [child] just as if she was my very own daughter. And I always kept that in mind. Whenever I would hesitate about disciplining her, I thought well, now, I know if* she was my very own or, you know, if I had had one I'd do this, and so I went right ahead and did it. So I just kept that in mind from the very beginning. And I did everything as if I'd had her from the first day she took her first breath.

Summary

Parents cited as advantages in adopting older children the fact that the parent age spread is more appropriate, the child is old enough so that he is capable of communicating with the parents and participating in family activity, and there is none of the drudgery of training and caring for a totally dependent infant. Less frequently given as an advantage was the fact that since the child had consciously experienced adoption the parent is not faced with the problem of informing him of it.

Additional advantages cited by a few parents were that adopting an older child permitted you to assess the child you were accepting; the children's immediate engagement in school and community peer activities mitigated strain on the parents' adjustment to the change of having a child, since care of the child was being shared with the school; also there was the special prestige in accepting for adoption a child whom, apparently, few others were ready to accept.

The parents felt a number of disadvantages were associated with the adoption of older children. Among those cited least was the danger that older children, being more easily recognizable and in contact with a greater number of people in the community, might be located by relatives or members of families with whom they had formerly lived.

Among the disadvantages listed with greater frequency were: the child comes to the family with some patterns of living already formed by other parental figures; the parent is deprived of some of the pleasures associated with caring for a baby; it is difficult to understand the child at times because, not having been with him during his earlier formative years, you are uncertain about the experiences which shaped his thinking and feeling, nor are you always aware of the details of his medical history. Since the child has lived with other families long enough to have developed some affectional ties to them, adoptive parents worry about competitive allegiance between the child's current living situation and memories of the past. Finally, there was the recognition that having lived under social and emotional stress for a long time it was to be expected that these children would bring emotional problems.

Adoptive parents coped with the problem of memories by being receptive to the child's desire to discuss this material, by permitting contact with past family members as an aid in helping the child to adjust to the transition, and by a patient confidence that the child would ultimately lift the emotional anchor from the former family and place it in the adoptive family. Children resolved the problem by ventilating feelings regarding past ties, by conscious suppression and "forgetting," and by repression; in a lesser number of instances children seemed not to have resolved affectional ties to the past, and in 14 of these cases the failure to resolve the problem occasioned conflict for adoptive parent and child.

In most instances, by the time we appeared for the interview, children had been living in the home for some time, the past had receded, and the impact of the need to live, act, interact, and respond in the parent had resulted in the development of strong bonds in the present at the expense of past memories. Symbolically all of the children had accepted a change in last names, and all were addressing the adoptive parents with appropriate parental titles, seemingly without conflict.

Children had manifested the gamut of the usual childhood emotional problems; enuresis was the problem showing the greatest incidence. They had displayed evidences of separation anxiety, the lack of trust which resulted from previous disappointing experiences with adults, and negative transference to adoptive parents. However these behaviors were manifested by only limited numbers of this group of children, although the potentialities for such behavior created by past experiences may have been present in all.

The general problem of discipline was discussed with specific reference to some of the particular problems and disadvantages occasioned by the need to discipline a child adopted when older. Parents face the problems resulting from the fact that the child has had experiences with different, and possibly inconsistent, approaches. The source of authority for the child has been diffuse since it was shared by foster parents, natural parents, and the agency. Both the child and the parent question the adoptive parent's entitlement to discipline. The need to discipline the child almost immediately arises without the opportunity of testing the effectiveness of different approaches and without knowing the consequences of previous discipline. Some modification is needed because of the atypical developmental history of these children, and some hesitancy may be occasioned by a desire not to deprive a child so often deprived in the past.

In general, however, despite the difficulties and despite the varieties of disciplinary approaches, most of the parents seemed to have coped effectively with the problems of discipline. The technique varied from family to family. The general feeling in applying discipline seemed to be less varied. The subjective impression was that in the greatest percentage of the families discipline was applied out of consideration of the child's needs and in an honest effort to do what was best for the child.

Adoptive parents who felt "entitled" to discipline, who approached disciplining problems with the feeling that the fact of adoption was irrelevant, seemed to be most comfortable in disciplining.

Chapter 8

SUMMARY

AND IMPLICATIONS

This chapter summarizes the study, introduces selective statistical data resulting from analyzing the relationship between background factors and outcome measures, makes explicit some general conclusions which derive from the study, and briefly discusses these conclusions.

This is a follow-up study of the experience of parents who adopted white, healthy, older children through one agency, The Division of Children and Youth, Wisconsin State Department of Public Welfare, over a ten-year period (1952–1962). The agency placed 150 such children who, at the time of adoptive placement, were older than 5 years of age but younger than 12. Of the total number of such placements 12 failed some time during the first year, and the child was removed from the home. In 138 cases legal adoption was completed. The 138 children included some multiple placements so that 112 families met all of the delimitations of the study. Failure to locate, movement out of the area, and refusal by one county judge of permission to contact the family reduced the number of the study sample to 95 families. Four families refused an interview, a rate lower than in most adoptive follow-up studies. The final study group, then, consisted of 91 families who met the delimitation of the study, were located, contacted, and who consented to partici-pate.

Data for the study were obtained from the agency records, joint interviews with the adoptive parents, and response forms completed by the parents at the end of the interview. The 2 to 3 hour interviews were tape recorded, only 4 families refusing permission for this. Typescripts of the interviews, averaging some 50 pages, were used as a basis for analysis of outcome by 3 typescript readers, all of whom were graduate social workers with experience in adoption.

Two criteria for outcome were developed. One was a compos-ite score of overall parental satisfaction in the adoptive experi-ence. This was derived by averaging independent judgments of the parents, the interviewer and each of the 3 typescript readers, all of whom used the same 5-level scale to assess the extent of parent satisfaction. The second criteria was the ratio of discrete satisfactions to dissatisfactions expressed by the parents in the interviews and identified by at least 2 of the 3 readers. The 2 measures of outcome were related to each other at a level beyond .001, and each gave slightly different overall percentages of successful outcome, but with neither method was successful outcome less than 82 per cent of the cases nor more than 87 per cent. The percentage of successful cases in this study was compared with other follow-up studies of adoptions. Despite the fact that the subjects of all of these studies were infant adoptions the level of success achieved was no different, in terms of statistical significance, from the level of success achieved with these older children.

The two outcome measures were consistently supported, in

the results they offered, by additional, supplementary data—parents' free response to sentence stubs requiring completion, as well as their replies to unstructured probes about advice they would give to friends regarding adoption of older children, and so on.

The children in this study group became available for adoption, in all instances, as a result of court action to terminate parental rights because of neglect and/or abuse. The families from which they came were atypically large, 52 per cent having 5 or more children. During their infancy they had lived in socially deprived circumstances, in substandard housing with families whose incomes were, most often, below poverty level. Natural parents had limited education, only 2 per cent of the fathers having completed high school. When employed they worked in unskilled or semiskilled occupational categories. The marital situation in the natural home was, in almost all instances, conflicted. In addition, the natural parents presented a picture of a considerable personal pathology compounded of promiscuity, mental deficiency, alcoholism, imprisonment, and psychosis. The mean number of specific social and personal pathologies exhibited by each of the natural families from which these children came was 5.7. Neither socioeconomic background of natural parents nor number of pathologies evidenced in the natural home was related to outcome.

The relationship between the natural parents and these children was most frequently characterized by physical neglect, although 31 per cent of the group were described as having experienced an emotional relationship which was "normally warm and accepting." Physical abuse was encountered in only 4 per cent of the mothers and 10 per cent of the fathers. The natural mother's relationship to the child when "normally warm and accepting" was highly related to outcome. However, a negative relationship to the child was not related to outcome. In only about 15 per cent of the cases was termination of parental rights actively opposed by the parents, and their attitude toward such termination was not related to outcome.

The group of children included 49 boys and 42 girls. Sex was not related to outcome. They were of average intelligence, had been removed from their own home at a mean age of 3.5 years, placed for adoption at the mean age of 7.2 years, and were at the mean age of 13.9 years at follow-up. They had experienced, on an average, 2.3 changes of homes prior to adoptive placement and throughout the period in placement had exhibited an average of 2.9 behavioral problems. The group as a whole, however, showed a greater degree of psychic health and stability than might have been anticipated given the nature of their backgrounds and developmental experiences. The child's capacity to develop interpersonal relationships, as assessed by the record readers based on the material included in the record by the social worker, was rated as "good" or "fair" in 79 per cent of the cases. "Capacity to develop interpersonal relationships" was highly related to outcome. The older the child was at time of placement (seen in the context of the fact that all these children were "older" by adoption standards) the greater the likelihood of less favorable outcome.

Outcome was related to the number of placements experienced, although it might be of interest to note that replacements were more frequently for administrative and/or situational reasons than because of child's unacceptable behavior in the foster home. The latter set of reasons accounted for only 19 per cent of the total replacements experienced by this group of children. The number of pathologies manifested by the child was, as expected, related to outcome. The more behavioral disturbances exhibited the less likely was outcome to be favorable. The child was "weaned," or "weaned" himself, gradually during placement from emotional attachments to his natural home and parents. The change in strength of such attachment was related to outcome, and when the child had not resolved such earlier ties, outcome was less likely to be favorable.

Since the older child, unlike the illegitimate infant placed for adoption, is likely to have developed a relationship with siblings, it is not unexpected to find that in 43 per cent of the cases these children were placed for adoption with siblings; this fact was not related to outcome.

The mean age of the adoptive mother at placement was 40 and of the fathers, 41.5. They are consequently older than most adoptive parents. However, the age difference between these adoptive parents is similar to the age difference between the more typical younger parents and their adoptive infants. Age of adoptive parents was not related to outcome, nor was religion of adoptive parents.

The adoptive parents were socioeconomically at a higher level than the natural parents, and almost all of these children were displaced upward in moving from their own to the adoptive home. Neither the degree of displacement nor the socioeconomic level of the adoptive parents was related to outcome.

In contrast to most adoptive parents a high percentage of the group (37 per cent) either had their own or an adopted child already in the home at time of placement. Previous experience as a parent was not related to outcome; nor was composition of the family at time of placement. Thirty per cent had previously been rejected as adoptive applicants, primarily because of age. As a group, these adoptive parents had experienced few developmental difficulties, but where such difficulties had been noted in the record it was not related to outcome.

Reasons for sterility was related to outcome. Where a woman had experienced miscarriages or where reason for infertility was not clearly established the likelihood was that outcome would be less favorable. While few parents preferred the older child at the point of placement, most were reconciled to the realities of the adoptive situation so as to be accepting of this. Reaction to the idea of adopting an older child was not related to outcome. While most of the parents reacted positively to the presentation of the child, reaction to presentation was not related to outcome. The largest percentage of the adoptive children and parents adjusted readily and without great difficulty to the placement, and in 75 per cent of the cases legal adoption was completed within the minimum period of time. In only 2 of the

91 families contacted did the adoption end in the child's subsequent removal from the home. In all other instances the child was still in the home at the time of the follow-up interview which took place on an average of 6 years after placement.

Outcome was positively related to parents' acceptance of the child, in their perception of him as a member of the family, and negatively related to self-consciousness by parents regarding adoptive status. However, very few of these parents were perceived as being self-conscious about their adoptive status. Almost all openly accepted their status as adoptive parents but at the same time felt there was little essential difference between biological and adoptive parenthood as this related to implementing parental roles in relation to the older child. Their perception of the community's attitude toward adoptive parents was essentially positive. There was no relationship between perception of community attitude as positive or negative and outcome.

Parents derived satisfaction from many areas: the child himself—his personality, temperament, mannerisms, and disposition; his achievements—artistic, athletic, social, educational—at school, in the community, with peers, and in the home; the parent-child relationship, companionship with the child, affectional responses from him, his obedience to, respect for, and sympathetic understanding of the parent, as well as in the child's pride in them, identification with and sharing of confidences. In addition, there was the occupation of parenthood itself as a lifelong interest, in the pleasure it affords in helping a child grow and develop, in successfully handling the problems of child rearing, and the appreciation it stimulates of the simple pleasures of life, as well as the opportunity to act as an exemplar to a dependent child. Additional sources of satisfaction were the positive relationship between the child and siblings and the child and the extended family, and the ability to resolve the problems of adoption. All were potential dissatisfactions as well. In aggregate, some 1,740 discrete satisfactions and dissatisfactions were identified by at least 2 of the 3 typescript readers as having been expressed by this group of parents. The overall ratio of satisfaction to dissatisfaction was 3.9 to 1.

Parents discussed some particular advantages of adopting the older child. The fact that the parent age spread is more appropriate for the older adoptive parent was mentioned most frequently (66 per cent). In descending order of frequency of mention were the following advantages: the child is old enough to do things with, there is none of the drudgery of training a totally dependent infant, the child is old enough to reason with, and because he consciously experienced adoption the parent is not faced with the problem of sharing this with him.

The parents talked about special problems in adopting the older child. The following were related to outcome measures: the fact that the child, having lived under stress, is apt to come to the adoptive home somewhat disturbed; he is difficult to understand because the parent has not shared a significant segment of his life; and he has been molded by others and in some measure "belongs" emotionally to others. Other special problems were mentioned but were not related to outcome: the disadvantage of missing the joy of having the child during his dependent infancy, the problems occasioned by lack of specific details regarding the child's health and developmental history. Despite the supposed separation between the child's adoptive family and his previous life, in 28 per cent of the cases these children had contact with "significant others" whom they had known in the past: foster parents, siblings in other homes, grandparents, etc.

The Reversibility of Trauma

The most significant general, overall conclusion of the study is that older children can be placed for adoption with expectation that the placement will work out to the satisfaction of the adoptive parents. The level of expectation of satisfying outcome is only slightly lower than that which might be anticipated in adoptive placement of infants.

The general conclusion is unexpected and raises a question of considerable interest. The data on the background factors and developmental history of these children, which was reviewed in Chapters 3 and 4 on the natural parents and the children, indicate that almost all lived, during early childhood, under conditions of social and emotional deprivation. The families into which they were born and from which they were removed by court action, after the community had recognized the dangers of such an environment for healthy child development, were characterized by considerable social and interpersonal pathology. The early lives of these children, who spent their most impressionable years under conditions of poverty, inadequately housed, with alcoholic, promiscuous parents who frequently neglected them, sometimes abused them, and only rarely offered them the loving care prerequisite to wholesome emotional development, make it difficult to explain the generally favorable outcome of these placements.

We echo the surprise expressed by some of the workers whose records we read in doing this study. One worker in her adoption summary statement said:

I think that this child will continue to make a good adjustment and to develop into a secure, happy child in an environment which can continue the permissive, understanding, and warmly accepting attitudes he has found in the receiving home. It is difficult, in view of the home environment from which the child came, and the type of separation which he has experienced, to account for the apparent lack of traumatizing and destructive influences in this picture. I cannot adequately explain where he might have developed his inherent ego strength and ability to accept normal and satisfying relationships, but I do feel that there is a remarkable amount of resiliency and ability in the child.

Before attempting an explanation, however, it might be well to point out that other studies have come to the same unexpected conclusion with similar expressions of surprise; in each instance the children studied turned out to be more "normal," less "maladjusted" than they had any right to be, given the trauma and insults to psyche experienced during early childhood.

Van Theis, in summarizing her impression derived from one of the first large scale follow-up studies of foster children, expresses some surprise at the adjustment of the group, 80 per cent of whom came from "bad backgrounds."

Our study of the group as a whole, insofar as the subjects have demonstrated their ability to develop and to adjust themselves to good standards of living, and perhaps even more strikingly, our study of individual members of it, leave us with a distinct impression that there exists in individuals an immense power of growth and adaptation. Our studies of these individuals and of the groups of individuals have shown that there were potentialities within these people which revealed themselves only under certain conditions. We would certainly not say that anything could be made of any child—that a favorable environment could produce any kind of development desired, but rather that our study leads us to believe that there are tremendous latent powers within an individual awaiting development, and that under favorable conditions these powers may be developed and directed toward accomplishment (80, p. 163).

Roe and Burks, both psychologists, did a follow-up study of 36 young adults who had, as children, been removed from their home and placed in foster care because their own parents were chronic alcoholics. Other types of deviant behavior were associated with alcoholism; 81 per cent of the fathers of these children "were guilty of mistreatment or neglect of their children"; 44 per cent of the mothers "mistreated or neglected their children" (73, p. 38). Since most of the children "became dependent as a result of court action—this means that the first few years of life of these children were spent in a home situation which left much to be desired—and that they were probably subjected to traumatic experiences during the early years of their lives" (72, pp. 382–83). The mean age at placement for the group was 5.6 years.

As adults, at the time of the follow-up interview, "most of these subjects have established reasonably satisfactory lives, in-cluding adequate personal and community relationships and most of them are married" (72, p. 388). When this group was contrasted with a group of adult former foster children who had come from "normal" homes broken by death and illness, it was noted that "there is no difference between the two groups in the percentage who feel reasonably secure and it does not appear that the proportion is much lower, if at all, than would be found in an unselected population" (72, p. 338).

Here, too, the authors are prompted to ask, "How did it happen that these children turned out as well as they did? How did it happen that in spite of these [adverse] factors many of them have become not only useful citizens but reasonably contented persons working adequately, with pleasant family lives and sufficient friends? No one who has read the records of some of these lives and pondered on them can escape a profound sense of awe at the biological toughness of the human species" (72, p. 391).

Maas conducted a follow-up study of 20 children who had been removed from home during infancy and early childhood and placed for at least a year in a residential nursery. He reviewed agency records, interviewed parents, and saw the children themselves, who at the time of the follow-up study some 20 years later were young adults. Maas reports that "although these 20 young adults may have been seriously damaged by their early childhood separation and residential nursery experiences, most of them gave no evidence in young adulthood of extreme aberrant reactions. . . . To this extent the data supports assumptions about the resiliency, plasticity and modifiability of the human organism rather than those about the irreversibility of the effects of early experience" (54, pp. 66–67).

In the follow-up study of independent adoptions conducted

by Witmer, a group of 56 children were identified as having lived under "possibly traumatizing conditions" prior to adoption. These children had lived under adverse physical conditions, and the psychological situation "was even more pathetic." At follow-up, there was little difference in the adjustment ratings achieved by this group of children as contrasted with other adoptees placed at a similar age and in similar adoptive homes but who had not experienced such "possibly traumatizing conditions" (91, pp. 286–87).

Meier completed a follow-up study of 61 young adults who had grown up in foster care. All of the group had experienced 5 years or more in foster care and none had returned to their own families. About half of the group had been removed from their own home before the age of 5. Between their first foster placement and their discharge from foster care at 18, these children had experienced an average of 5.6 living arrangements. Most of them had been removed by the courts from their own homes "In which they had experienced inadequate care" (55, p. 197).

Based on lengthy interviews with the group, now young adults, Meier concludes that "the vast majority of the subjects have found places for themselves in the community. They are indistinguishable from their neighbors as self-supporting individuals, living in attractive homes; taking care of their children adequately, worrying about them, and making some mistakes in parenting, sharing the activities of the neighborhood and finding pleasure in their association with others" (55, p. 206). Meier says: "Child welfare workers are continuously baffled, as well as heartened, by the fact that over and over again they see children removed from impossibly depriving circumstances who, by all the rules 'ought' to be irreparably harmed, who, nevertheless, thrive and grow and learn to accept love and affection and respond to it" (56, p. 12).

Rathbun reported on a follow-up of 33 foreign children who, after having suffered considerable deprivation in their own country, were placed for adoption in the United States. Interviews by case workers with the adoptive parents 6 years after placement, supplemented by contact with the schools, showed that "the adjustment of the majority was judged adequate and in some cases notably superior" (67, p. 6). The report concludes by noting that "the consistence of the ratings for all categories in which assets outweigh liabilities, points in the direction of a considerable degree of reversibility of the effects of early psychic damage" (67, p. 131). Another research group studied 22 Greek children institutionalized during the first 2 years and subsequently placed for adoption in the United States. Testing and interviews, 5 years after adoption, rated only 2 of the children as "poorly adjusted. . . . We can conclude, therefore, that despite early deprivation the children have done remarkably well" (68, p. 19).

Welter studied 72 children placed for adoption in America when older than 5 years of age. Thirty-six of the group were born outside America and transferred to that country for adoption. Some 85 per cent of the children were judged to be showing "good" to "excellent" adaptation on follow-up (88, Table 40, p. 126).

Welter notes, in summarizing her report, that "perhaps the single most important implication may be drawn from the fact that according to the social workers [responsible for working with the children] both of these groups of older adoptive children . . . , despite extended exposure to massive deprivation, have indicated a degree of responsiveness to a restitutive environment and a reversibility of early psychic damage which seems to exceed even the most optimistic assessments of the studies on maternal deprivation and separation we have seen thus far" (88, p. 164).

A follow-up study by Tinker (83) of 112 emotionally disturbed children in foster care indicated that "when basic needs are met many of these disturbed children do outgrow some, or all of their behavior and personality problems." Evaluation at follow-up was made in terms of the child's adjustment at home and school and in the community as reported by caseworkers, foster parents, and others familiar with the child's behavior.

Most of the children in the study "had spent their early formative years in homes disorganized by desertion, alcoholism, immorality or other forms of social breakdown."

Heston studied the effects of institutional care on adult adjustment. Hospital, school, police, and armed forces service records were used in addition to personal interviews and Minnesota Multiphasic Personality Inventory. Three psychiatrists independently gave each subject a mental health rating in terms of a mental health sickness rating scale formulated by the Menninger Clinic. The general conclusion was that the "long term effects of childhood institutional care are much less drastic than had been feared." In explanation of the findings the researchers point out that "the factor most clearly related to the effects of institutional care as seen in the subjects of this report is the corrective experience of family living—it appears that the human organism has the happy capacity of reversing the effects of childhood emotional trauma of the type connoted by institutionalization" (32, p. 1109).

If the studies reviewed by Bowlby (7) in his widely disseminated and influential report point to the dramatic negative effects of early trauma, it might be significant to call attention, in this context, to the fact that, as Yarrow reminds us (92, p. 20), a sizable proportion of the children in each of the studies listed did not show the predicted negative reactions to separation and deprivation.

While the studies cited above vary in precision of methodological approach one might note, as did Bowlby, that "What each individual piece of work lacks in thoroughness, scientific reliability or precision is largely made good by the concordance of the whole" (7, p. 15).

The idea of irreversibility of trauma is related to the continuity hypothesis. This presupposes that the disturbed child will become the disturbed adolescent, who then becomes the disturbed adult. Studies by Robbins (70), Morris (57, pp. 743–54, 58, pp. 991–97), and Livson and Peskin (48, pp. 509–18) tend to suggest that the hypothesis needs further refinement and specification. Children manifesting neurotic symptoms very frequently become well-adjusted adults. Childhood antisocial behavior, while outgrown in some cases, is more likely to lead to maladjustment in adulthood. As Kohlberg (40) notes, however, there is no linear relationship between childhood diagnosis and adult prognosis.

Factors Relating to Reversibility

Does the above then imply a contradiction of the most important tenets of child rearing: that continuous contact with one set of loving, accepting, understanding parents providing the proper emotional as well as physical support is the best basis for healthy biopsychosocial development? We are not suggesting that neglect, abuse, and physical deprivation are not harmful. Each of the studies cited above shows that a more detailed contrast within the follow-up group invariably favors subsets of children with a more benign environment prior to separation. For instance, while most of the children in the Maas study and most of those in the study by Roe turned out reasonably well adjusted, those who came from less pathological backgrounds did better than those who had been subjected to more trauma (54, p. 67, 72, Table 1, pp. 381–2). In the present study, outcome is related to natural mother's acceptance. Nor do the results contradict the objection that while these children may have achieved normal levels of functioning they may not, because of early deprivation, have realized their full psychosocial potential. There is no way of knowing what levels of functioning these children might have achieved if they had had a continuous positive experience from birth.

The data does not argue for a rejection of the generally accepted tenets but rather refinement of such principles and a qualification of them. It argues, it seems to me, for a recognition that children have varying capacities to deal with potentially traumatic conditions and that these strengths enable them, when provided with a healthier environment, to surmount the damaging influences of earlier developmental insults.

Social and emotional childhood deprivations may be the necessary preconditions for later maladjustment; for some they are not sufficient conditions. Certain children possess greater capacity for recovery from hurt. Others may be less vulnerable, so that situations which are damaging to most children affect them less adversely. What is generally regarded as traumatic may be merely annoying, irritating, and inconvenient to them. The core of self remains relatively undamaged.

In the balance between what the child brings and what the environment has to offer, we have developed the conviction that what the environment offers, or fails to offer, is by far the major determinant of developmental outcome, and that early environment is of crucial importance. Yet the outcome for the very deprived children in this study and outcome for similar groups of children who were the subject population of studies cited above suggest giving greater consideration to what the child brings to the environment and greater weight to the influence for change of a later, healthier environment.

Empirical evidence supports such an explanation of the unexpected outcome of this and similar studies. Studies of differences between children immediately after birth, before one can say differences are due to the effects of variations in their surroundings, indicate that children differ in many ways which have significance for the resultant of interaction between themselves and their environment. Thus, Thomas studied 130 children from the first months of life onward. From the moment of birth, children differed in terms of activity, adaptability, distractability, persistence, mood, intensity of reaction to sensory stimuli, threshold of responsiveness, and so on. He notes that

all infants will not respond in the same fashion to a given environmental influence. Rather, given constancy of environmental factors the reaction will vary with the characteristic of the child upon whom the relatively constant stimulus is brought to bear. . . . This holds true for all aspects of the child's functioning . . . including reactions to situations of special stress, such as illness, radical change in living conditions or abrupt shifts in geographic environment. . . . This view of the child stands in contrast to the assumption that environmental influences, as such, have determinative effects. . . . Underlying the environmental approach is the assumption that all children will tend to react similarly to the same developmental influences. . . . Our findings suggest that exclusive emphasis on the role of environment in child development tells only part of the story and that responses to any regimen will vary in accordance with primary patterns of reactivity (81, pp. 84–5).

Similarly, Dr. Wagner Bridger, director of a longitudinal team study of 300 children from birth, at the Albert Einstein Medical College, concludes—as a result of the research thus far —that "the role of environmental variables in growth and development has to be evaluated in the context of the biological endowment of the individual" (47, p. 134). These conclusions are supported by additional research which points to the same fact: that children are different at birth in ways which are crucial for personality development (20, 25, 90).

If biological determination of individuality, as contrasted with environmental or experiential determination of individuality, is given greater consideration, the resiliency of the children in this study group may be more explicable. One child's trauma, which makes future positive adjustment very improbable, may be another child's inconvenience, the effects of which, given reasonable opportunity, can be reversed.

Such research concerned with biological differences in vulnerability to trauma, capacity to adapt to trauma, and levels of resiliency and "recoverability" in the face of trauma is perhaps one general approach to explaining the contradiction between anticipated outcome, given the pathology in the background of these children, and the outcome in response to placement in an adoptive home which met the child's essential needs.

However, there may be another, more sociological explanation. These children made 2 important shifts in moving from their own home to the adoptive home. They made the change, referred to above, from a home which offered little in the way of meeting their needs in terms of affection, acceptance, support, understanding and/or encouragement to the adoptive home which offered some measure of these essential psychic supplies.

They also made a change from a lower-class, multiproblem family in a slum to a middle-class reputable home in an area of the community which had some status. A child's self-concept is developed as a result of his experience in the intense relationship with significant others within the intimacy of the family group, particularly in relation to the most significant of all others, the parents. A child who perceives himself as acceptable to the parents perceives himself as acceptable to himself.

But however important this factor is in building the child's self-concept, it ignores the impact of the wider world which soon begins to transmit messages to the child which affect his conception of self. The Negro child has to have a much stronger positive self-image, initially, to withstand the corrosion on this image of the thousands of overt and covert cues which come from the predominantly white environment, all of which say black is bad, white is better.

The white child with an initially shaky self-concept, supported, reinforced, and strengthened by an environment which affirms his acceptability, is likely to end up with a more positive conception of self than is a Negro child born into a loving, accepting family which gives him, initially, a strong self-concept subsequently denied by a society which manifests its open rejection of him.

This problem operates along class lines as well as along color lines. The same kind of messages are received by subsets within the white community. The standard bearers of the white community behave toward the lower-class, multiproblem, disreputable white family so as to transmit the message that they are unacceptable. The child in such a family, carrying its name and associating with its members, inevitably begins to be affected by this pervasive, negative labeling.

We then remove the child from this family and place him in an apparently decent, middle-class home in an attractive neighborhood, and identify him with a well-organized family of father and mother who act in a responsible, respectable manner. He now receives messages which proclaim his acceptability, and support, reinforce, and strengthen whatever components, however limited, of self-acceptance he has been able to develop as a result of whatever small amount of affection he received in his former home. The effect of positive parent-child relationships within the home are now buttressed by social relationships outside the home rather than vitiated by the contradiction between the acceptance of the lower-class child in the lower-class home and his rejection by the community.

Burks and Roe, in attempting to explain the better-than-anticipated outcome in foster care of children removed at an average age of 5 from homes in which the parents were alcoholic and/or psychotic, point to this as a factor which needs consideration.

Had these children remained with their own outcast families, they, too, would have been, in a sense, outcasts. The children of respectable families would, in all likelihood, not have been permitted to play with them. They would not have had the kind of clothes the other children had; they would not have been invited to their parties; and nasty remarks about their fathers and mothers would have been shouted after them on the street. They could react only by identifying with their families and rejecting the community and all its customs, or by rejecting their families and striving ceaselessly somehow to achieve membership in the group which had despised them.

The children were removed from such homes and placed in acceptable ones, and the authors note that:

It seems very probably that residence in a home which is a respected part of the community, and the child's acceptance as a member of that community, make possible the formation of an organized ideal derived from the attitudes and forms of behavior of the community which can function as an integrating force . . . (73, p. 116).

Srole, in his report of a large-scale effort to assess the level of "mental health" of people in midtown Manhattan, reports that the mental impairment was related to socioeconomic level. More of the "poor" were apt to be "mentally impaired." In attempting to explain this, the report points to the factor of community rejection of the lower-class child which intensifies tendencies toward maladjustment. "In many areas of his experience the lower class child encounters the contempt, implicit but palpable, in the non-verbal behavior of others who think of him in the symbolism of such words as rubbish, scum, dregs, riffraff and trash. These devastating judgments inevitably force their way into his own self-evaluating processes" (79, p. 198).

In moving the child from a lower-class home and social environment to a middle-class adoptive home and social environment the agency has "rescued" him from a situation which intensifies the problem of adjustment to one which assists the making of a positive adjustment. A recognition of these factors —the factor of biological potential providing a resiliency which permits the child, despite past deprivation, to make a healthy response when provided with a healthy environment, and the implication of a changed social context which reinforces, rather than opposes, change in the child toward a more positive adjustment—has implications for adoptive practice in addition to providing some reasons for unanticipated results.

Social workers, together with mental hygienists, have tended to overemphasize the importance, significance, and power of the past. Although we say that the past is structured in the present and is *one* of the determinants of present behavior, we tend to see the past as more powerful than the present and the most significant determinant of present behavior. History, despite the historian's interest in the past, favors a situational psychology. Hitler transformed a nation in a decade so that there were few to support a democratic ethos; southerners, who only yesterday swore not to ride in desegregated buses and eat in desegregated restaurants are doing that today. The situation, the living context in which one lives and with which one is forced to come to terms, demands a mobilization of those latent aspects of ego which are congruent with situational demands; contrariwise, it forces a defense against those aspects of ego which make adjustment to the situation difficult, hazardous, and precarious.

We may need a reorientation in emphasis with a greater respect being accorded the present and the more recent, proximate experiences. The past does, of course, intrude to shape perception, and in the case of the psychotic and seriously neurotic it may even be decisive. But for those less ill, which includes the children in the present study as well as most children available for adoption, the present is a countervailing force which exerts a constant pressure, demanding that we live in response to it.

The whole rationale of therapy presupposes that experience in the present can free us from the past. The provision of a different environment, social class, neighborhood, and family is perhaps the most therapeutic of all therapies for a child. The new living situation offers the opportunity for making manifest the potential for changed feeling and behavior.

This point of view is supported by the results of other recent follow-up adoption studies. Analysis of the data of one study, obtained through tape-recorded interviews with 200 adoptive families, showed that only one of the many background factors regarding the adoptive child and his early developmental experience was related to the level of success of the adoption (43, p. 163). Detailed agency records made available developmental information such as age at adoption, preadoptive placement history, psychological evaluation, and rating of emotional deprivation. These background factors showed remarkably little relationship to later functioning. Whatever experiences the child may have encountered earlier seems to be compensated for by the experience of living in a good adoptive home. The study notes that "it appears very much as though background variables take on less and less impact as prognostic factors through the passage of time. . . . With time, in a relatively normal family setting, the children are free to gain, and realize, their basic potential" (36, pp. 149–50).

A recent follow-up study of 160 Negro and white children showed no significant relationship between such background factors, such as child's age at adoptive placement, number of preadoptive placements, early behavior of the child, and adjustment at follow-up (69, p. 485). The researchers conclude that "in general, factors pertaining to the child and particularly those used to assess potential risks to development, did not prove discriminating" (69, p. 496).

For the children whose lives were carefully reviewed in both these studies, the preadoptive past seems to have been of less importance and significance for determining adjustment than the experiences in the adoptive present. Adoption is not psychotherapy. But its psychotherapeutic potential is like that of a good marriage, a true friendship, a new satisfying job, on an enjoyable vacation. It can help to repair old hurts.

The child could not make of himself what he was not. However, personality is multifaceted, and we are capable of a much greater repertoire of behavior than we are generally called upon to manifest. The altered situation, requiring a "change" in personality for the child, means an emphasis on the kinds of feelings and behavior which helped him fit in to the adoptive home and a de-emphasis of those kinds of feeling and behavior unacceptable in the present environment.

What is involved here are different approaches to an explanation of what is psychotherapeutic. The rationale basic to the traditional social work approach to therapy (specific remedial measures) suggests that the behavior itself is not of primary importance since it is merely a manifestation of some underlying intrapsychic conflict. Since behavior is merely symptomatic of underlying disturbances these inner causes, rather than the behavior itself, should be the focus of attention. The behavior itself is purposive and beyond rational control, simple reeducation, exhortation or persuasion since the individual is motivated to act in this way in response to a conflict which he cannot resolve because its nature is not fully available to conscious awareness. Changes in behavior may be achieved, but unless the basic conflict is resolved, other, equally disabling, symptoms may be substituted for the symptom which is no longer manifested.

It would be futile to seek to change behavior and/or relieve symptoms without attempting to trace and resolve the conflict, the "real" problem, from which the symptoms originate. It follows then that effective therapy is directed not toward changing behavior but toward achieving understanding, toward an "expansion of consciousness" so that it includes the hidden sense of conflict. "If the client can be helped to understand why he behaves as he does or to recognize and understand the origin of his neurotic tactics that continually defeat him, he will gradually abandon the inappropriate behavior and substitute therefor more rational tactics in the management of his life" (34, p. 474). The promotion of self-understanding and insight is the most effective approach toward helping people with their problems, and all strategies—reassurance, universalization, desensitization, catharsis, clarification, and interpretation—are valued because they free emotional energy or change the balance of intrapsychic force so as to maximize the possibility for self-understanding. Even environmental manipulation, reducing, modifying, and mitigating external stress infringing on the client, is regarded as a desirable tactic primarily because this, too, frees ego energy (previously devoted to struggling with the environment) for dealing more effectively with the basic intrapsychic conflict. These postulates are fundamental to one view of what is psychotherapeutic deriving primarily from psychoanalytic psychology.

Another view of therapy follows from the learning and conditioning psychologies. Here, the primary concern is with the behavior itself without concern for underlying "causes." The behavior is viewed as the result of some unfortunate learning and conditioning experiences which have taught undesirable, unadaptive approaches to interpersonal relationships. "The concept of symptoms," as a response to an underlying conflict, in this view is unnecessary and superfluous (82, p. 8).

Here therapy focuses primarily on the behavior itself; it is concerned with providing an opportunity for "unlearning" the unadaptive behavior and learning new, more adaptive modes of behavior. The therapy seeks to identify "unsuitable stimulus-response connections," to dissolve them and to teach more desirable "stimulus-response connections." It seeks to identify the specific environmental conditions through which the undesirable behavior is controlled and sustained and to change these. The stress is on immediate experience and specific behavior.

Our view of what is therapeutic about adoptions is closer to the second rationale for therapy outlined, the learning-conditioning rationale, than it is to the first—the psychoanalytic psychology rationale.

The child's previous living experiences may have "taught" a view of parents and parental surrogates which resulted in neurotic, unadaptive behavior. Defenses were developed and behavior manifested which was in response to the nature of the situation to which the child was subjected. Moving into the adoptive home meant moving into an environment which was set up to condition the child to a change in behavior. Previously learned, now inappropriate, behaviors went unrewarded or were actively discouraged; new, more appropriate, more adaptive behaviors were rewarded and actively encouraged. Without any explicit effort to resolve whatever underlying intrapsychic conflict may or may not have been present, without any explicit effort to have the child develop insight or self-understanding into his distorted perception of himself in the parent-child relationship and/or his distorted expectations with reference to the parents' behavior toward him, the living experience provides the corrective in day-to-day learning. The living experience teaches new ways of relating to people and new ways of perceiving oneself. In this sense, life is therapeutic. It acts as a large-scale conditioning matrix which stimulates and supports changes in the child's feeling and behavior. As Franz Alexander says, "No insight, no emotional discharge, no recollection, can be as reassuring as accomplishment in an actual life situation in which the individual has failed" (1, p. 40).

Psychotherapy is, in effect, a condensed, systematic attempt to imitate curative, real life situations and assure the availability of such a curative configuration to the patient. Environmental therapy—therapy which actually affords the child the opportunity to live in a healthier family situation and experience the possibility of successful interaction with parents—is, as Josslyn notes, "the least artificial form of therapy" (36, p. 120).

The curative resource, the adoptive home, is made available as the result of the institutionalization of an area of concern such as the field of child welfare in the profession of social work. The resource itself is the regenerative force, and while the effectiveness of the resource in application in each individual instance may be increased or diminished somewhat by the work of the individual practitioner, it is the availability of the resource itself which is of prime importance.

By far the most important thing the social agency does for the child is to provide him with an adoptive home. All else is commentary. All the casework preparation, all the casework efforts in easing transition, all the casework in follow-up during the post placement year is frosting on the cake of the potential for change provided by a different environment. The agency achieves its supreme importance in making available a responsible, formally organized channel for bringing together the adoptive home and the child needing such a home. In the case of this group of children studied here, providing this change in environment for the child was social work's greatest contribution. The agency arranged the living situation of these children so that they were offered a therapeutic environment—a healthy restitutive living experience. The social agency, the institutionalized apparatus sanctioned and supported by the community, made it possible for the community to identify the children needing help, to act to remove the children from a clearly damaging situation, and then to find adequate substitute homes for these children. It made available a formally organized channel through which people interested in adoptive children could apply and be received with understanding. If it had not been for the social workers engaged in this work, some percentage of the children might never have found a home, and some percentage of the parents would never have found these children. This is the true and ultimate contribution of the social agency; that it was instrumental in making available to the child a second chance at growing up, this time in a reasonably healthy environment.

If the therapeutic potential of such a situation is so rich, if the therapeutically beneficient present reacting with the child's capacity for a healthy response offers fertile possibility for positive change, then the agency should take greater risks in moving more expeditiously to place children. Discharging the community mandate with a sense of professional responsibility would still require that the agency make a careful selection of children for placement and of parents to receive them; it would still require that the agency prepare both parents and children carefully to mitigate the inevitable problems which arise in the difficult transition as strangers meet to become a new family. But it might temper caution with the recognition that children are perhaps capable of more positives than they have ever been able to actualize, and that these may never become manifest unless the child is given the opportunity of living in an adoptive home. It might temper caution by the recognition that the only way the child can be made ready for adoption is to be given the opportunity of living as an adopted child. No amount of preparation for marriage can achieve what is achieved by the experience of being married. Similarly, the child in living adopted becomes adopted. A sense of responsibility might be tempered by an optimistic orientation toward the positive potentials of the adoptive situation, as such, for evoking what both parents and children can offer, if given the chance, to make the adoption a success.

We have come to realize that expectations are a powerful force in determining outcome. The self-fulfilling prophecy, the placebo effect, and the Rosenthal effect (71) all point to this same phenomenon. Every adoptive placement is an experiment. If the social worker communicates an expectation of success this, in itself, is a factor which increases the likelihood of success of the placement. The study suggests that we can justifiably communicate expectation of success.

In a symposium on the adoption of Oriental children in American homes, one of the participants said:

I think we need a gambling attitude or a probability attitude towards our work. We need to think in terms of probability chances. We might try thinking of probability chances, with a big role given to the unknown factors. But I think part of the fault lies in our own evaluation standards. We're always looking for 100 per cent success. I would prefer to set up as a criterion of success in an agency the fact that there is a percentage of failures of a given size. We want a certain per cent of failures (if we have a selection of cases) before the agency is considered to be doing its job. It means that the agency has accepted risky cases and extended itself for maximum service in the selection, and has not eliminated those cases which are unsure. A small loan company area manager said that he rates his area office not on the fact that they may have zero or a very small percentage of failure of repayment of loans. He claimed that there had to be certain percentage of failures to repay, because otherwise the district manager was playing too conservative a game, and was not developing the proper range of business. He was turning down fair risks as well as poor risks! The same point of view might probably hold for the evaluation of a social agency (11, pp. 56–57).

Perhaps this is the most important result of the study. Agencies can take the risk in placing of older children with a high probability of success. Some failures are inevitable. But unless it takes the risks, a sizable number of children, however pessimistic a prognostication one might make from background data, will be denied the opportunity for a therapeutic experience to which they can respond. The agency—and the parents —accepting the risk will have rescued these children for life.

But the results have implications beyond the adoptive agency and the adoptive family. The adoptive child is first a child and secondly an adoptive child; the adoptive family is first a family and secondly an adoptive family. All children in all families face the possibility of injury, illness, and death of parents. Many children must adjust to family conflict which often leads to divorce, separation, or desertion. Life gives no guarantees to any child, anywhere, that life will be without trauma, without limited or prolonged periods of separation from parents, without hurts. The results speak, then, to all children, in all families, who at all times face the possibility of some measure of deprivation. And the results suggest that a child's resiliency and capacity for adaptation very often enable him to struggle effectively and successfully with the tragic circumstances of life. Despite the inevitability of tragic circumstances, many children have emerged from such struggles reasonably healthy, reasonably happy, reasonably well-adjusted people.

REFERENCES

1. Alexander, Franz; French, Thomas. *Psychoanalytic Therapy.* W. W. Norton and Co., New York, 1946.
2. Armatruda, Catherine; Baldwin, Joseph. "Current Adoption Practices," *Journal of Pediatrics,* Vol. 38, February 1951.
3. Ball, Betty. "Identification Problems of Adopted Children," *Smith College Studies in Social Work,* Vol. 35, October 1964.
4. Bell, Velma. "Special Considerations in the Adoption of the Older Child," *Social Casework,* Vol. 40, June 1959.
5. Bernard, Viola. "First Sight of the Child by Prospective Parents as a Crucial Phase in Adoption," *American Journal of Orthopsychiatry,* Vol. 15, April 1965.
6. Boehm, Bernice. *Deterrents to the Adoption of Children in Foster Care.* CWLA, New York, December 1958.
7. Bowlby, John. *Maternal Care and Mental Health.* World Health Organization, Geneva, Switzerland, 1951.

8. Brenner, Ruth. "A Follow-up Study of Adoptive Families," *Child Adoption Research Committee*, New York, March 1951.
9. Brown, Florence. *Adoption of Children with Special Needs*, CWLA, New York, March 1959.
10. ———. "Supervision of the Child in the Adoptive Home," *Child Welfare*, Vol. 34, March 1955.
11. Child Welfare League of America. *Adoption of Oriental Children by American White Families—An Interdisciplinary Symposium*, CWLA, New York, 1960.
12. Citizens Adoption Committee of Los Angeles County. *Our Children in Foster Homes—A Study of Children Needing Adoption*, Los Angeles, California, 1953.
13. Colville, Anita. "Adoption for the Handicapped Child," *Child Welfare*, Vol. 36, October 1957.
14. Colvin, Ralph. "Toward the Development of a Foster Parent Attitude Test," in *Quantitative Approaches to Parent Selection*, CWLA, New York, January 1962.
15. Davis, Ruth M.; Douck, Polly. "Crucial Importance of Adoption Homes Study," *Child Welfare*, Vol. 34, March 1955.
16. Dukette, Rita; Gerard, Margaret. "Techniques for Preventing Separation Trauma in Child Placement," *American Journal of Orthopsychiatry*, Vol. 24, January 1954.
17. Dyer, Everett D. "Parenthood as a Crisis: A Restudy," *Marriage and Family Living*, Vol. 25, May 1963.
18. Edwards, Jane. "The Hard-to-Place Child," *Child Welfare*, Vol. 40, April 1961.
19. Edwards, M. E. "Failure and Success in the Adoption of Toddlers," *Case Conference*, Vol. 1, November 1954.
20. Escalona, Sybelle K. *The Roots of Individuality*, Aldine Publishing Co., Chicago, 1968.
21. Fairweather, O. E., "Early Placement in Adoption," *Child Welfare*, Vol. 31, 1952.
22. Fanshel, David. "Measuring Adjustment in Adoptive Parents," in *Quantitative Approaches to Parent Selection*, CWLA, New York, January 1962.
23. Fradkin, Helen. "Adoptive Parents for Children with Special Needs," Discussion by Ruth Taft, *Child Welfare*, Vol. 37, January 1958.

24. Fradkin, Helen; Krugman, Dorothy. "A Program of Adoptive Placement for Infants under 3 Months," *American Journal of Orthopsychiatry*, Vol. 26, 1956.

25. Fries, Margaret; Woolf, P. "Some Hypotheses on the Role of the Congenital Activity Type in Development," *Psychoanalytic Study of the Child*, Vol. 8, International Universities Press, New York, 1953.

26. Gochros, Harvey. *Not Parents Yet—A Study of the Postplacement Period in Adoption*, Division of Child Welfare, Minnesota Department of Public Welfare, Minneapolis, Minnesota, 1962. Mimeo 1688.

27. Gorden, Henrietta. *Casework Services for Children*. Houghton Mifflin Co., Boston, Mass., 1956.

28. Graham, Lloyd. "Children from Japan in American Adoptive Homes," *Casework Papers*, 1957, FSAA, New York, 1957.

29. Hallinan, Helen. "Adoption for Older Children," *Social Casework*, Vol. 33, July 1952.

30. _____. "Who Are the Children Available for Adoption," *Social Casework*, Vol. 32, April 1951.

31. Hastings, James, Editor. *Encyclopedia of Religion and Ethics*. Charles Scribner's Sons, New York, 1908.

32. Heston, L. L.; Denny, D. D.; and Pauley, I. B. "The Adult Adjustment of Persons Institutionalized as Children," *British Journal of Psychiatry*, Vol. 112, 1966.

33. Hobbs, Daniel. "Parenthood as a Crisis—A Third Study," *Journal of Marriage and Family Living*, Vol. 27, August 1965.

34. Hobbs, Nicholas. "Sources of Gain in Psychotherapy," in *Interpersonal Dynamics*, Bennis, Warren G.; Schein, Edgar H.; Berlew, David E.; Steel, Fred. I Edition, The Dorsby Press, Homewood, Illinois, 1964.

35. Hylton, Lydia F. "Trends in Adoption, 1958–1962," *Child Welfare*, Vol. 44, July 1965.

36. Josslyn, Irene. *Psychosocial Development of Children*. Family Service Association of America, New York, 1948.

37. Kadushin, Alfred. "The Legally Adoptable, Unadopted Child," *Child Welfare*, Vol. 37, December 1958.

38. _____. "A Study of Adoptive Parents of Hard-to-Place Children," *Social Casework*, Vol. 43, May 1962.

39. Kadushin, Alfred. *Adopted but Unplaced Children under Guardianship to the Wisconsin State Department of Public Welfare, Division of Children and Youth.* Unpublished, 1958.
40. Kohlberg, Lawrence; LaCross, Jean; Ricks, David. "The Predictability of Adult Mental Health from Childhood Behavior," in B. Wolman, Editor. *Handbook of Child Psychopathology,* McGraw-Hill Book Co., New York, 1970.
41. Krause, Mignon. "New Horizons in Adoption," *Child Welfare,* Vol. 36, April 1957.
42. Krugman, Dorothy. "Reality in Adoption," *Child Welfare,* Vol. 43, July 1964.
43. Lawder, Elizabeth A.; Lower, Katherine D.; et al. *Post-placement Functioning in Adoptive Families, A Follow-up Study of Adoptions at the Children's Aid Society of Pennsylvania.* Final Report to the Children's Bureau, R-114, August 1966 (mimeo).
44. Lawder, Elizabeth A. "A Limited Number of Older Children in Adoption—A Brief Survey." *Child Welfare,* Vol. 37, November 1958.
45. Leatherman, Anne. "Placing the Older Child for Adoption." *Children,* Vol. 4, May–June, 1957.
46. Le Masters, Ersel, "Parenthood as a Crisis," *Marriage and Family Living,* Vol. 19, 1957.
47. Levin, Phyllis. "There Are Babies and Babies," *New York Times Magazine,* September 19, 1965.
48. Livson, N.; Peskin, H. "The Prediction of Adult Psychological Health in a Longitudinal Study," *Journal of Abnormal and Social Psychology,* Vol. 72, 1967.
49. Lyle, Leon. "Placing Older Children for Adoption," *Child Welfare,* Vol. 28, January 1949.
50. Lynch, Elizabeth; Mertz, Alice. "Adoptive Placement of Infants Directly from the Hospital," *Social Casework,* Vol. 36, December 1955.
51. McWhinnie, Alexina M. *Adopted Children—How They Grow Up.* Routledge and Kegan Paul, Ltd., London, 1967.
52. Maas, Henry; Engler, Richard. *Children in Need of Parents.* Columbia University Press, New York, 1959.
53. _____. "The Successful Adoptive Parent Applicant," *Social Work,* Vol. 5, January 1960.

54. ———. "The Young Adult Adjustment of Twenty Wartime Residential Nursery Children," *Child Welfare*, Vol. 42, February 1963.

55. Meier, Elizabeth. *Former Foster Children as Adult Citizens.* Unpublished Ph.D., Columbia University School of Social Work, 1962.

56. ———. "Current Circumstances of Former Foster Children," *Child Welfare*, Vol. 44, April 1965.

57. Morris, H. H.; Soroker, Eleanor; Burrus, Genette. "Follow-Up Study of Shy Withdrawn Children—I. Evaluation of Later Adjustment," *American Journal of Orthopsychiatry*, Vol. 24, 1954.

58. Morris, H. H.; Escoll, P. J., Wexler, R. "Aggressive behavior disorders of childhood: A follow-up study," *American Journal of Psychiatry*, Vol. 112, 1956.

59. Morrison, Hazel. "Research Study in Adoption," *Child Welfare*, Vol. 29, 1950.

60. National Association of Social Work. *Social Work Encyclopedia*, NASW, New York, 1965.

61. National Association for Mental Health, England. *A Survey Based on Adoption Case Records.* NAMH, London, 1954.

62. Nelson, Doris. "A Follow-up Study of the Adjustments of 15 Adopted Children," *Smith College Studies in Social Work*, Vol. 35, October 1964.

63. Nieden, Margarete Z. "The Influence of Constitution and Environment upon the Development of Adopted Children," *Journal of Psychiatry*, Vol. 31, 1951.

64. Nordlie, Esther; Reed, Sheldon. "Follow-up on Adoption Counseling for Children of Possible Racial Admixture," *Child Welfare*, Vol. 41, September 1962.

65. Pennypacker, Kathryn S. "Reaching Decisions to Initiate Court Action to Free Children in Care for Adoption," *Child Welfare*, Vol. 40, December 1961.

66. Polier, Shad. "Amendments to New York's Adoption Law— The 'Permanently Neglected' Child," *Child Welfare*, Vol. 38, July 1959.

67. Rathbun, Constance; et al. *Later Adjustments of Children following Radical Separation from Family and Culture.* Paper

presented at the Annual Meeting of the American Orthopsychiatric Association, Chicago, 1964.

68. Research Institute for the Study of Man. *Final Report to Children's Bureau on Study of Adoption of Greek Children by American Foster Parents*, R-22, November 1964, mimeo, New York.

69. Ripple, Lilian. "A Follow-up Study of Adopted Children," *Social Service Review*, Vol. 42, December 1968.

70. Robins, Lee N. *Deviant Children Grown Up*. The Williams and Wilkens Co., Baltimore, Maryland, 1966.

71. Rosenthal, Robert. *Experimenter Effects in Behavioral Research*. Appleton-Century-Crofts, New York, 1966.

72. Roe, Anne. "The Adult Adjustment of Children of Alcoholic Parents Raised in Foster Homes," *Quarterly Journal of Studies on Alcohol*, Vol. 5, June 1944–March 1945.

73. Roe, Anne; Burks, Barbara. "Adult Adjustment of Foster Children of Alcoholic and Psychotic Parentage and the Influence of the Foster Home," *Memoirs of the Section on Alcohol Studies*, No. 3, Yale University, 1945.

74. Schechter, Marshall D. "Observation on Adopted Children," *A.M.A. Archives of General Psychiatry*, Vol. 3, 1960.

75. Shapiro, Michael. *A Study of Adoption Practice*, Vol. III, *Adoption of Children with Special Needs*. CWLA, New York, April 1957.

76. Shaw, Lulie. "Follow-up Adoptions," *British Journal of Psychiatric Social Work*, No. 8, November 1953.

77. State Charities Aid Society. *Adoptability—A Study of 100 Children in Foster Care*. Child Adoption Service, New York, 1960.

78. Starr, J. "Adoptive Placement of the Older Child," *Casework Papers*, NCSW, Columbia University Press, New York, 1954.

79. Srole, Leo, et al. *Mental Health in the Metropolis—The Midtown Manhattan Study*. McGraw-Hill Book Co., New York, 1962.

80. Theis, Sophie Van. *How Foster Children Turn Out*. State Charity Aid Association, New York, 1924.

81. Thomas, Alexander; Birch, Herbert; Chess, Stella; Hertzig, Margaret; Korn, Sam. *Behavioral Individuality in Early Childhood*. New York University Press, 1963.

82. Thomas, Edwin J.; Goodman, Esther. *Socio-biological Theory and Interpersonal Helping in Social Work.* University of Michigan, School of Social Work, Campus Publishers, Ann Arbor, Michigan, 1965.

83. Tinker, Katherine. "Do Children in Foster Care Outgrow Behavior Problems?" *Minnesota Welfare,* Vol. 8, Nos. 4, 5, 6, October, November, December 1952.

84. U.S. Children's Bureau. *Supplement to Child Welfare Statistics 1967—Adoptions in 1967.* Statistical Series No. 92, U.S. Government Printing Office, Washington, D.C., 1968.

85. U.S. Department of Commerce. *Statistical Abstracts of the U.S.—1963.* U.S. Government Printing Office, Washington, D.C., 1963.

86. U.S. Department of Health, Education and Welfare. *Dictionary of Occupational Titles,* Vol. I, Second Edition. Federal Security, U.S. Government Printing Office, Washington, D.C., March 1949.

87. Weinstein, Eugene. *The Self Image of the Foster Child.* Russell Sage Foundation, New York, 1960.

88. Welter, Marianne. *Adopted Older Foreign and American Children.* International Social Service, New York, 1965.

89. Winch, Robert F. *Mate-Selection—A Study of Complementary Needs,* Harper & Brothers, New York, 1958.

90. Witkin, H. A.; et al. *Psychological Differentiation.* John Wiley & Sons, New York, 1962.

91. Witmer, Helen; Herzog, Elizabeth; Weinstein, Eugene; Sullivan, Mary. *Independent Adoptions.* Russell Sage Foundation, New York, 1963.

92. Yarrow, Leon. "Maternal Deprivation—Toward an Empirical and Conceptual Reevaluation," in *Maternal Deprivation,* New York, January 1962.

93. Young, Leontine. *Wednesday's Children.* McGraw-Hill Book Co., New York, 1964.

INDEX